Books by Daniel Glen Van Straten

I Could Go On and On

    Book One, *Schemer*
    Book Two, *Boone*

Boone

The Further Adventures of Schemer

Daniel Glen Van Straten

Book Two of
*I Could Go On and On:
A Librarian Remembers*

Glen Outlook Publishing

Published by

Glen Outlook Publishing
3633 S 17th PL
Sheboygan, WI 53081

Copyright ©2009 by Daniel G. Van Straten
All rights reserved. No part of this book may be reproduced in any form or by any means, electronic or mechanical, without permission.

First printing 2009

Illustrations by Daniel Glen Van Straten.
Portraits by Leiningers of DePere, Wisconsin, and F.J. Pechman of Appleton, Wisconsin, copied with permission as noted.

Library of Congress Control Number: 2009903210
ISBN: 978-0-578-02834-7

Publisher's Cataloging-In-Publication Data
(Prepared by The Donohue Group, Inc.)

Van Straten, Daniel Glen.
  Boone : the further adventures of Schemer / Daniel Glen Van Straten.
     p. : ill. ; cm. -- (I could go on and on : a librarian remembers ; bk. 2)

  Includes bibliographical references.
  ISBN: 978-0-578-02834-7

1. Van Straten, Daniel Glen. 2. Librarians--Wisconsin--Biography. 3. United States--Social life and customs--20th century. 4. United States. Army--Military life--20th century. 5. Dutch Americans--Genealogy. I. Title.

Z720.V36 I38 2009 bk. 2
020.92   2009903210

Printed in the United States of America

Writing this book gave me a chance to share my life's story, a family heritage, a life vocation, memories, turning points, cherished traditions, and dreams.

I have written this book for my daughter Kaye, my son Kurt, my grandson Eric, and all other descendants.

I dedicate this book to my beloved wife Ervida, my parents Aloysius and Cecilia, my brothers Roger, Gerald, Donnie, Lennie, Russell, and Carl, my sisters Joyce, Alice, Karen, and Mary, my cousins, aunts, uncles, all posterity, including my friends and associates, and my high school agriculture teacher and class advisor Marvin Obry. All of these have been influential and present in my life, of utmost importance.

My father Aloysius had the curiosity of not just one cat but hundreds of cats. He was an avid reader and learned, and had the desire to learn new things just to know about them. My mother Cecilia was a good listener and encouraged me to make my own decisions as long as they were good ones. Marvin Obry became principal of Shiocton High School and later administrator at the Hortonville schools and continuously stressed the importance of education. My aunts Grace and Erna were strong motivators. All of these people motivated me in persevering to succeed with my educational endeavors and achieving the pursuit of happiness.

Preface

Throughout my lifetime I have longed to write about my life and adventures.

After reading my first book, family members and friends asked if I intended to write a second book. Most requested it. I wasn't able to let them down. I have so much to share.

Family, ethnic heritage, and tradition have played an important part in my life. Friends and associates became as close as family.

As Schemer I skipped from one event or adventure to another. It was the same way with Boone.

This book is about my life in college and in the army and finding romance, but it also covers eventful happenings in the Bovina Township. Hunting, fishing, and travel were an important part of my life and of my family.

In order to fully understand the saga of my series, *I Could Go On and On*, the reader needs to have read my first book, *Schemer*. The story continues on and on from one book to another, and most pictures and drawings are not repeated.

Original drawings and photographs add meaning to my writing and help tell my story.

I published my book in book format and CD format and with good reason. It costs too much to print a book with colored pictures, but creating a CD with colored pictures is affordable. The book and the CD are the same, except the book contains black and white pictures in grayscale and the CD colored pictures. The CD is a computer disc. A CD-ROM drive and Adobe Reader are needed to read the CD disc. Read the book, look at the CD's colored pictures.

Contents

Preface xiii
Acknowledgments

Part One **In Titans Land, 1957-1961**
    They Called Me Boone 5
    Getting Ready for College 9
    The End of the Fabulous Fifties 17
    The Swinging Sixties 25
    I Am Dutch, I Am German 37
    The De Groots 43
    The Summer of '57 49
    OSC 53
    Getting My Feet Wet 59
    A Gullible Greenhorn 69
    The Summer of '58 85
    A Rebounding Sophomore 91
    The Summers of '59, '60, and '61 109
    A Traveling They Did Go 119
    A Fishing They Did Go 125
    Hunting the Big Ones 131
    A Frazzled Junior 143
    To Be or Not To Be 155

Part Two I'm in the Army Now, 1962-1964
     The Missouri Ozarks   169
     The Mountain Post   191

Part Three Back in Titans Land, 1965-1967
     Back Home   223
     Sinterklaas   235
     A Scattering of Dutch Sayings   239
     Proverbs of Other Lands   241
     After the Wildlife   249
     Go Pack, Go!   257
     Sands Through the Hourglass   265
     An Enchanting Halloween   271
     A Whiz of a Senior   285
     A Library Interview   297
     My Favorites   301
     Errata: Corrections on the *Schemer* Facts   311
     Praise for *Schemer*   313

Acknowledgments

Very special thanks to:

My daughter Kaye Ervida Van Straten and cousin Donna Remmert for igniting a spark in me to write my story.

My wife Ervida Van Straten for her patience, love and understanding throughout my writing.

My brothers Roger, Gerald, Russell, and Carl Van Straten, my sister Mary Van Kirk, and my wife Ervida Van Straten for their constructive critique of the first draft of the text.

Leiningers of DePere, Wisconsin, and F.J. Pechman of Appleton, Wisconsin, for their permission to copy and reproduce selected portraits in digital format. Photo courtesy rendered with each portrait.

Sources:
    Aloysius L. Van Straten. *My Autobiography*. 1976.
    "Leonard & Wilhelmina Van Straten Family Tree."
        <July, 2006>.
    U.S. Army Training Center Engineer, Fort Leonard
        Wood, Missouri. 1962.
    Quiver 1958-1959. Oshkosh State College,
        Oshkosh, Wisconsin.
    Quiver 1960-1961. Wisconsin State College at
        Oshkosh, Wisconsin.

Quiver 1967. Wisconsin State University at Oshkosh, Wisconsin.
Farewell Shioc High. 1996.
Dictionary of 1000 Dutch Proverbs. Edited by Gerd de Ley. 1998.
The Concise Oxford Dictionary of Proverbs. [Compiled by] John Simpson with the assistance of Jennifer Speake. 1992.
The Prentice-Hall Encyclopedia of World Proverbs. [Compiled by] Wolfgang Mieder. 1985.

Boone

Part One

In Titans Land, 1957-1961

They Called Me Boone

Instead of being called by our birth names, many of us were branded with nicknames.

When I was a young boy, I was called Schemer. My high school teacher Ivan White and Aunt Edna called me Danny. Many called me Dan. Ma and Pa and my siblings all called me Daniel. Aunt Nona called me Daniel in the Lion's Den. A few years after graduating from high school, I was called Boone, and the name stuck with me the rest of my life.

Many of my friends and relatives got branded with nicknames, too.

My brother Lennie, we called Jim.

My brother Russell, we called Dutch.

My sister Karen Mary, we called by her second name Mary until sister Mary was born.

My sister Joyce Elaine Josephine, we often called by her second name, Elaine.

My brother Gerald, we called Gug.

My mother Cecilia (birth name Celia), shortened to Cele.

My dad Aloysius, shortened to Al.

My cousin Jacqueline, we called Jackie.

My cousin Robert Brownson, we called Bob Joe.

My friend John Beyer, we called Porky.

My nephew Darrell, we called Bones.
My nephew Wayne, we called Ace.
My nephew Duane, we called Peenie.
My grandma Wilhelmina, we called Minnie.
My niece Donna, we called Poogie.
My aunt Frances, we called Sis.
My cousin Willard Last, we called Sonny.
My niece Sharon's husband John Hintzke, we called Snap.
My brother Carl's wife Barbara, we called Bobbie.
My aunt Agnes Brownson, we called Dolly.
My grandpa Len's brother Henry, we called Hank.
Hank's daughter Frances, we called Tootie.
My aunt Rosa, we called Hootsie. She became a nun with the name of Sister Lurana Marie, but we often continued to call her Hootsie.
Dwight D. Eisenhower came to be known as Ike.
John Fitzgerald Kennedy was called Jack or J.F.K., and his brother Robert Francis Kennedy they called Bobby or R.F.K.
Buildings, institutions, and things also got nicknames or shortened names, often referred to as initialisms. The University of Wisconsin was called UW. Oshkosh State College was OSC. Restrooms became known as "the can." To stop to use the restroom was called "a pit stop."

MEMORIES

I remember taking the SATs.
I remember our junior class prom, "Blue Hawaii."
I remember Joyce's class ring.
I remember getting class rings.
I remember being on the graduation honor guard.
I remember a class trip to a Milwaukee Braves game.
I remember eating in a Chinese restaurant on a class trip to Chicago.
I remember our senior class play, Finders Creepers.
I remember high school graduation.

Getting Ready for College

We, the graduating class of 1957, were getting ready for the next stage of our lives. Some were going to college, some joining the military, some getting married, and some getting a full-time job. No matter what our plans, it was a time of challenge, excitement, and adventure.

During our junior year (1955-1956) our adventures embodied the high school achievement tests, the college entrance tests (ACTs), the scholastic aptitude tests (SATs), and the junior prom.

Everyone had to take the high school achievement tests. The college bound student had to take the SAT (Scholastic Aptitude Test) or the ACT (American College Test) or both. Most colleges accepted ACT scores for entrance but not all accepted the SAT. These tests required the use of special pencils to fill in tiny squares for our answers. They were timed, and the teacher monitoring the test told us when to start and when to stop. We got a short break between the parts of the test. I have no idea of how I scored on the tests. I passed and nothing else mattered.

Many school activities occurred throughout the year,

like the football games, the Homecoming bonfire, game, and dance, the basketball games, the thrilling rides on the bus to the away games, the class plays, the field trips, and the student dances, but the junior prom was the big event of the year. Once the basketball season ended, all our energies centered on the junior prom. We called our junior prom "Blue Hawaii." The big day was April 27, 1956. Cousin Dick Van Straten was prom king and Barbara Waterstradt reigned as prom queen. The prom court of honor included cousin Mike Van Straten, Len Guyette, and Kay Kuether. Margo Bergstresser was my date. We decorated the gym with streamers of crayon paper, posters, and a water fountain. We got excused from classes to practice marching around the gym in preparation for prom night. To march around the gym in an imaginary Hawaiian theme excited everyone. Cousin Margy Miller added a bit of class to the event with her Hawaiian dance.

    Another exciting happening during our junior year was getting class rings. Joyce wore her class ring continually. All the letters, numbers, and insignia had worn off. I wanted to wear a class ring, too. Ma and Pa let me buy one. Some rings had black onyx, some red, some white. I wanted to get red, but it cost too much, so I had to settle for black onyx. The ring manufacturer placed the 57 digits for the year of graduation on the ring, with the 5 on one side and the 7 on the other side. Our name initials were put on the ring, too. The initials DS were put on my ring. I preferred DV but didn't ask to have it changed because of the cost. Now as I look at my class ring, I am glad I got black onyx. Black is actually a terrific color.

    We read and analyzed some great literary works in our high school English classes, like *Julius Caesar*, *Silas Marner*, and *The Scarlet Letter*. This helped prepare those of us college bound to analyze literary works.

Lois Poeschel   **Juanita Heinonen**

English teacher Miss Lois Poeschel and history teacher Miss Juanita Heinonen engaged us in a writing project with emphasis on history and grammar. I chose the War of 1812, and earned an A on this writing project. I learned to take notes from resources on 3 x 5 inch cards and to write my paper from those notes. The writing techniques I learned in this project provided me with the basis of preparing all my future theme papers.

I visited Oshkosh State College (OSC) during my junior year of high school and decided OSC was going to be the college I attended. Some Shiocton High School graduates went there, and it wasn't far from home.

Brother Russell was attending OSC for his third year and shared his OSC experiences with us. Russell brought home OSC. When he studied the fruit fly in his collegiate genetics class, Russell brought the culture home with him. He needed to study the genetic structure and reproduction of the fruit fly. The only problem was some of the flies got loose in the house as Russell experimented with them.

A great happening occurred at the end of my junior year in high school. I was selected to be on the graduation honor guard with three other junior classmates, Dave Shier, Marilyn Hinz, and cousin Norita Van Straten. This was a great distinction. We escorted the senior graduates into the gymnasium with lighted candles and sat in the front row during the graduation ceremony. At the end of the ceremony we handed roses to the graduates and followed them out.

Susie Kruzicki

Mrs. Susie Kruzicki performed the duties of chief cook. She had many helpers, including aunt Erna Warning and brother Roger's wife Gerry. Susie used lots of butter. Her three layer casserole of hamburger, mashed potatoes, and sauerkraut was a favorite. The students enjoyed many a meal prepared by Mrs. Kruzicki.

Carol Sommers

Cousin Carol Sommers performed the duties of school secretary. Carol supported me with the teachers. She motivated my biology teacher Mr. Rickaby to allow me to finish a test on bones. Mr. Rickaby let me finish it, and I scored a 100 on it.

Brothers Roger and Gerald drove school bus. They alternated with each other between driving the school bus and taking care of the filling station. Other bus drivers included George Jones, Ken Fredricks, Harold Anthony, Bob Hanks, Clayton Allender, Don Little, and wife Zetta Little.

During my senior year (1956-1957) I worked on getting the paperwork done in the school office for attending OSC. I received a needy scholarship towards my tuition costs.

Brother Roger and family lived in the house just east of the filling station. I stopped over to see Gerry during school lunch hours.

We went on class trips to Milwaukee and Chicago. Some of us ate in a Chinese restaurant in Chicago. Visiting Chicago was enlightening. We viewed skyscrapers, walked through sliding doors, and met people of a different colored skin. Most of us went to the Milwaukee Braves baseball game in Milwaukee. They played against their rivals the New York Yankees. Hank Aaron and Warren Spahn were the big draw.

The senior class play, *Finders Creepers*, took up our time between the basketball season and the prom. We didn't do tryouts. Our senior English teacher Mr. Charles Niles had

Charles Niles

us read the play in English class and assigned our roles based on the readings. I lucked out with one of the major parts. I wore Pa's white nightgown dyed red and pranced back and forth in it on the stage. I had a big surprise at the end of the year on senior awards night-- Mr. Niles presented me with the drama award. I was shocked to say the least, and it was totally unexpected.

    We thoroughly enjoyed our last days as seniors at Shiocton High School. The senior class was put to work in the last few days before senior awards night and the graduation ceremony. We had to set up the bleachers on the stage before senior awards night with cement blocks and lumber. The school administrators allotted us a big portion of a day for signing class yearbooks and exchanging class pictures. All the teachers were eager to sign. Marching in and out during the graduation ceremony in our navy blue graduation gowns turned out to be an awesome experience. It felt so good to be graduating and moving on with our lives. We marched to the tune of "Pomp and Circumstance," played by Mrs. Don Ronk. I had butterflies in my stomach as we marched in and out to this tune. I think this is one of the best pieces of music ever composed.

    A wonderful year! A great adventure! After all, I am an Aries, and Aries the Rams are great adventurers.

MEMORIES

I remember Ike and Mamie.
I remember the movie, Ben Hur.
I remember the Milwaukee Braves baseball team.
I remember shaking Bill Proxmire's hand.
*I remember when the Golden Arches first came on the
     scene.*
I remember the Barbie doll debut.
I remember the TV quiz show, "The $64,000 Question."

The End of the Fabulous Fifties

"I like Ike," cried the American people. Dwight Eisenhower, elected to a second term in 1956, winning by a great margin over Adlai E. Stevenson, continued to be popular not only with the Republicans but with everyone. America loved Ike's wife Mamie, too. In 1959 near the end of his second Presidential term, Alaska and Hawaii became new states. Richard Nixon served as Vice-President during Ike's Presidencies. In 1958 Nixon was spat on and had stones thrown at him in Peru and Venezuela.

On the cost of living scene, a new home cost $10,950; a new car, $1,910; a movie ticket, 75 cents; rent, $87 per month; gas, 23 cents per gallon; a postage stamp, three cents; milk, 93 cents per gallon; bread, 18 cents per loaf; and, a new TV set, $99.95. The average income earned was $4,137.

The Chevy Impala debuted and became a popular buy.

De Gaulle took over power in France.

Robert Earl Hughes, a man known to be the world's heaviest human being weighing in at 1,067 pounds, died in 1958 at the age of 32.

Khrushchev became the supreme ruler of the Soviet Union. He was denied a visit to Disneyland.

Liz Taylor was the gossip of the town. Eddie Fisher divorced Debbie Reynolds and married Liz in 1959, but the marriage only lasted a few years. Actually, Liz has had seven husbands and has been married eight times. She married Richard Burton twice. All of her marriages ended in divorce, except for the one to Michael Todd. He died in a plane crash. The other husbands were Conrad Hilton, Michael Wilding, John Warner, and Larry Fortensky. Liz had two boys with Wilding and a daughter with Todd.

Taylor is remembered for her adolescent roles in the movies *Lassie Come Home, National Velvet,* and *Little Women.* Later she had adult roles in the movies *Father of the Bride, A Place in the Sun, Cat on a Hot Tin Roof, Raintree County, Cleopatra,* and *Suddenly, Last Summer.* She won best actress academy awards for her roles in *Butterfield 8* and *Who's Afraid of Virginia Woolf?* Liz was a beautiful actress and had a passion for jewelry. She has been a close friend and supporter of Michael Jackson.

As far as the other gender goes, Paul Newman had become a popular draw at the movies. He starred with Liz Taylor in Tennessee Williams' *Cat on a Hot Tin Roof* (1958), after having portrayed boxer Rocky Graziano in the 1956 film, *Somebody Up There Likes Me.* Some of his other major films included: *The Helen Morgan Story* (with Ann Blyth) (1957), *The Long, Hot Summer* (with wife Joanne Woodward) (1958), *The Hustler* (1961), *Hud* (1963), and *Cool Hand Luke* (1967).

Newman raced autos at Elkhart Lake during the 1970s and 1980s. He developed a passion for racing autos after filming at Road America in Elkhart Lake, WI.

People were reading as evidenced in the sale of over 350 million paperback books. The most popular books included Boris Pasternak's *Doctor Zhivago* (also made into a movie), Art Linkletter's *Kids Say the Darndest Things,* and Vladimir Nabokov's *Lolita.*

Teen-agers continued to be the biggest fans of pop music.

TOP HIT TUNES OF 1958-1959

"Volare" (Domenico Modugno)
"It's All in the Game" (Tommy Edwards)
"Patricia" (Perez Prado)
"Rockin' Robin" (Bobby Day)
"Johnny B. Goode" (Chuck Berry)
"Do You Want to Dance?" (Bobby Freeman)
"Tom Dooley" (The Kingston Trio)
"All I Have to Do is Dream" (The Everly Brothers)
"Chantilly Lace" (The Big Bopper)
"Devoted to You" (The Everly Brothers)
"('Til) I Kissed You" (The Everly Brothers)
"La Bamba" (Richie Valens)
"Lonely Boy" (Paul Anka)
"Mr. Blue" (The Fleetwoods)
"May You Always" (The McGuire Sisters)
"Oh, Lonesome Me" (Don Gibson)
"Splish Splash" (Bobby Darin)
"Teen Angel" (Mark Dinning)
"Some Enchanted Evening" (*South Pacific*)
"Thank Heaven for Little Girls" (*Gigi*; Maurice Chevalier)

Jack Paar reigned on the "Tonight Show."
Pope Pius XII died, and the Vatican elected John XXIII as Pope.
Vanguard, a U.S. satellite, was launched.
Sweden's Ingemar Johansson took the world's heavyweight title away from Floyd Patterson.
Big movie hits included *Ben-Hur, The Sound of Music*, and *Green Mansions*. *Ben-Hur* won 11 Oscar awards in 1959, including Best Picture and Best Actor (Charlton Heston).
Another great movie watched over and over again was

All Mine to Give, also known as *The Day They Gave Babies Away.* It was a tear jerker. The story took place in Eureka, WI. When his Scottish parents died, their 12-year-old son had to be strong like an adult and take on the difficult task of finding homes for his five younger brothers and sisters.

The Braves came onto the Milwaukee arena in 1953 with Eddie Mathews and Warren Spahn winning National League highs. Hank Aaron, an unproven infielder, became a rookie outfielder and helped the Braves finish in third place in 1954. The Braves had another winning season in 1955, finishing in second place. During the 1956 season Hank Aaron obtained the batting title. They came back to win the National League Pennant in 1957, with Hank Aaron as MVP and Warren Spahn winning the Cy Young. The Braves won their second straight National League Championship in 1958. They were unable, however, to get a third World Series win in 1959.

Racism entered the sports arena. It is shocking to know sports games were cancelled because of racism and segregation. It hit right at home in Wisconsin with the UW Badgers football team. Games were cancelled between the Badgers and Louisiana State University (LSU) in 1957 and 1958 because the State of Louisiana outlawed Black people from participating in social events and athletic contests. Only whites were allowed admission to the Sugar Bowl in New Orleans. Since they were not going to leave their Black players home, the Badgers changed their playing schedule to play other teams. LSU was undefeated in 1958 and won the national championship, but the Badgers coach believed the Badgers were capable of defeating LSU in 1958 if only the Black players had been allowed to play. The civil rights movement gained impetus in 1959, and the U.S. Supreme Court ruled Louisiana's segregation law to be unconstitutional. African-Americans and whites were once more able to compete together in the games in all arenas.

After many attempts to become Wisconsin's Governor, William Proxmire was elected to the U.S. Senate in 1957, filling the Senate seat vacated by Joseph R. McCarthy. He served the State of Wisconsin in the U.S. Senate until 1989.

Proxmire became noted for many things during his lifetime. He was a poster child for health and fitness. He graduated from Yale and Harvard. He gave a speech each day the Senate met and set roll call records. Bill turned down campaign contributions. He was an avid newspaper reader and loved doing crossword puzzles. He rose early to exercise and jogged five miles to work no matter the weather. He wrote seven books, all published. He detested vacations. After several years of being bald, Proxmire underwent painful hair transplants. He also had a face lift. He was the most disciplined person you ever met.

Proxmire's Golden Fleece awards were his trademark. He toiled against government waste (like Federal spending on chauffeurs), wasteful military spending, and useless research studies (like the $27,000 project on why prisoners escape). He also worked hard on finance and credit reforms and for an anti-genocide treaty.

Proxmire got personal with the American public and with Wisconsinites. His name was a household word. He showed up at the Wisconsin State Fair's main gate and flower building, shaking hands as people entered saying, "I am Bill Proxmire." He did the same at the Green Bay Packers games. I shook his hand.

The Golden Arches came on the scene. McDonald's stands started popping up all over the country, selling 15-cent burgers and 10-cent fries. McDonald's became very popular because society was ready for it. People were more mobile and leading busy lives. More women worked, and mothers were hustling kids to and fro. It was convenient to grab some hamburgers and French fries at McDonald's in a jiffy instead of wasting time in a restaurant.

Do you believe it? A Barbie doll! Barbie measured 11 ½ inches tall, and the day of her debut occurred on March 9, 1959 in the fictitious town of Willows, Wisconsin. She was much cooler than other dolls because she had curves and wore fabulous clothes. Barbie first appeared as a fashion model with a pony-tail, wearing a black-and-white striped strapless bathing suit, sunglasses, hoop earrings, and black open-toed heels. Yes, this was Barbie Millicent Roberts, and she had a boyfriend named Ken Carson. She was destined to be a flight attendant, ballerina, teacher, and astronaut on several occasions. Barbie had over one billion pairs of shoes, 22 dogs, 15 horses, seven cats, a parrot, giraffe, zebra, and chimpanzee.

The TV quiz show "The $64,000 Question" attracted many viewers. Pa enjoyed watching it and so did the rest of us in the family. Contestants chose a subject category, such as boxing or cooking, and then were asked questions on the category, with earned money for correct answers doubling ($1, $2, $4, $8, $16, $32, $64, $128, $256, $512, $1,000, $2,000, $4,000, $8,000, $16,000, $32,000, $64,000). After $4,000, the contestant returned each week for one question. The contestant was able to quit at any time with their earnings. If a question was missed before $8,000, no prize was awarded. If a question was missed after $8,000, a consolidation prize of a new Cadillac was given. At the $8,000 level, the contestant occupied an isolation booth and only heard the quiz show host.

One contestant, a Black American girl, had to spell a lengthy word in the isolation booth. She paused between each letter. The word correctly spelled was A-N-T-I-D-I-S-E-S-T-A-B-L-I-S-H-M-E-N-T-A-R-I-A-N-I-S-M. She spelled it right. This intrigued all of us. We looked for the word in the dictionary. Actually, the one whole word didn't appear in the dictionary, but we found a listing for "disestablishment" and one for "arianism" and then the prefix "anti." The entire word probably appeared all together in one of the big unabridged dictionaries. Anyway, we determined what the word meant-- a movement opposed to the separation of church and state.

"The $64,000 Question" ended November, 1958. It turned out to be a scam. It was rigged. What a disappointment. One contestant said he received the answers during his screening. All the other TV quiz shows also got cancelled. All credibility was lost. The television networks now switched from quiz shows to westerns.

POPULAR TELEVISION SHOWS OF 1958-1959

"The Real McCoys"
"The Danny Thomas Show"
"I've Got a Secret"
"The Life and Legend of Wyatt Earp"
"Have Gun Will Travel"
"Wagon Train"
"Gunsmoke"
"The Rifleman"
"Maverick"
"Tales of Wells Fargo"

MEMORIES

*I remember tie-dyes, herb teas, the Beatles, the Supremes,
     sexual freedom, lower hemlines, stricter gender roles,
     and the disconcerting girdle.*
*I remember JFK and Jackie, Lyndon and Lady Bird, and
     Humphrey.*
I remember the assassinations and the riots.
I remember the hippie generation.
I remember the top hits and the TV shows.
I remember sex and killings being included in movies.

The Swinging Sixties

Smoking and the Cold War characterized the sixties. Men dreamed of owning a home in the suburbs, a happy home with a beautiful wife and children. Women were still mostly homebodies. They had to take care of the home and the kids.

The sixties was a period of social change, such as the civil rights movement, feminism, and gay rights.

John Fitzgerald "Jack" "J.F.K." Kennedy campaigned for President under the Democratic ticket, with Lyndon Baines Johnson as his running mate. Russell and Carl saw Kennedy when he gave a campaign rally in our area. He was elected President in 1960, winning by a close margin, defeating Richard Milhous Nixon, the Republican nominee, following a highly publicized television debate.

Jacqueline "Jackie" Kennedy married Jack Kennedy in 1953, and they had four children. Two died early, leaving Caroline and John J. "J.J." America loved Jack, Jackie, Caroline, and J.J. Women loved Jackie's style, grace, and hair style.

Kennedy advanced the space program, plugged in tax cuts, and started the Peace Corps. To make Americans active citizens, Kennedy said: "Ask not what your country can do for you; ask what you can do for your country."

Kennedy commanded a PT boat during the Second

World War and exhibited a great amount of bravery when his boat got rammed and sank.

Jack was the youngest man ever elected President and the first and only Roman Catholic elected President to date.

Soon after Kennedy took office, the Cuban Crisis surfaced. First the Bay of Pigs Invasion occurred when Cuban exiles tried to invade the homeland. It didn't succeed. Next, Kennedy blockaded the Island of Cuba in 1962 when Russia tried to install nuclear missiles there. He further demanded Russia to remove the missiles and reduce military forces in Cuba.

A man named Lee Harvey Oswald assassinated J.F.K. on November 22, 1963. Jack and Jackie were riding in an open vehicle in a Dallas, Texas Presidential tour, and Oswald shot Jack in the head from a window in the Texas Textbook Depository Building.

The Nation mourned a slain President, and the world grieved. This put the Cold War on hold for a few days.

As Oswald was being transferred to another jail, a man named Jack Ruby shot him. Ruby got ill and died before going to trial.

Within 98 minutes of Jack Kennedy's death, Lyndon Baines Johnson was sworn in as the thirty-sixth President of the United States.

President Johnson continued with Kennedy's measures of a civil rights bill and a tax cut. On July 2, 1964, Johnson signed the Civil Rights Act of 1964. On August 6, 1965, he signed the Voting Rights Act, reinforcing the 15th Amendment ratified about 95 years earlier.

Johnson was elected President again in 1964 and served to 1969. Johnson's programs included: aid to education, urban renewals, conservation, and fighting poverty. The Vietnam War was a thorn in Johnson's side, and he didn't seek election for a second term because of it.

Richard Milhous Nixon became our thirty-seventh President in 1969. I was just a few feet away from him at a campaign rally in Sheboygan, Wisconsin. He defeated Hubert Humphrey in the election. Nixon completed the withdrawal of U.S. troops from Vietnam.

Jackie married Aristotle Onassis in 1968, and it lasted until 1975.

More killings and assassinations occurred after John Kennedy's.

Martin Luther King Jr., a Baptist minister and leader of the American Civil Rights Movement, led the Montgomery Bus Boycott and the 1963 March on Washington, delivering his famous "I Have a Dream" speech. His speech established King as the greatest speaker in American history. He committed himself to the driving forces of love, peace, family, equality, human dignity, freedom, and self respect. King received the Nobel Peace Prize in 1964.

Demonstrators marched from Selma, Ala. to Montgomery, Ala., on March 7, 1965, pressing for voting rights. Police officers stopped them at the Edmund Pettus Bridge with whips, clubs, and tear gas, hospitalizing 50 marchers. This encounter, known as "Bloody Sunday," won support for a voting rights law becoming a reality five months later.

King was assassinated on April 4, 1968 by a sniper, James Earl Ray. Dr. King had delivered another famous speech the day before he died, " I See the Promised Land," also known as "I've Been to the Mountaintop." In 1986 America began celebrating Martin Luther King Jr. Day as a national holiday. Only a few other individuals have had this honor bestowed upon them, i.e. Christopher Columbus, Abraham Lincoln.

Robert Francis "Bobby" "R.F.K." Kennedy, a younger brother of John Kennedy, served as U.S. Attorney General from 1961 to 1964. He became one of President Jack Kennedy's closest advisors. R.F.K.'s best work had to be the Civil Rights Movement. After serving as U.S. Attorney General, R.F.K. was elected U.S. Senator. He severed ties with

President Johnson on the Vietnam War. As he campaigned for President in 1968, Bobby was shot. A national day of mourning followed his death.

The U.S. Surgeon General's report on smoking came out in 1964.

The summer of 1967 turned out to be a summer of love and a summer of racial tension, civil disturbances, and riots. The Black man had poor housing and was subjected to brutal police shootings. Civil rights activists concentrated on fair housing issues. Father James Groppi led many fair housing demonstrations. It took 200 days of marching to get approval of a fair-housing ordinance. The rioting and demonstrations worsened so much as to cause curfews to close taverns, liquor stores, and gas stations. The streets were cleared and road blocks appeared.

At the same time as the riots and demonstrations occurred, the youngest generation rebelled against the social norms of the day. It was the time of the hippie generation. More demands were made for freedoms and rights for women, gays, and minorities. Drug use and psychedelic music characterized this social revolution. An anti-war movement surfaced. It became the time of the draft dodger and conscientious objector.

The space race was on. Spending increased in science and technology. In 1961 the Soviets orbited the Earth and the USA came up with Project Apollo. In 1969 America won the race with Apollo 11 as American astronauts Neil Armstrong and Buzz Aldrin walked on the moon.

The Pontiac GTO, Plymouth Barracuda, Ford Mustang, and Chevrolet Corvette surfaced as the newest sports cars. The telephone industry introduced touch-tone phones in 1963. Sony marketed the first video tape recorder in 1965. The first heart transplantation occurred in 1967.

The motion picture industry released many popular movies. The social taboos of sex and violence broke up with the start of the cultural revolution. Movies now included harmful shootings and sex scenes.

GREAT MOVIES OF THE SIXTIES

The Hustler, **starring Paul Newman (1961)**
Lawrence of Arabia, **starring Peter O'Toole (1962)**
The Manchurian Candidate **(1962)**
To Kill a Mockingbird, **starring Gregory Peck (1962)**
What Ever Happened to Baby Jane? **Starring Bette Davis and Joan Crawford (1962)**
Cape Fear **(1962)**
Days of Wine and Roses **(1962)**
Lolita **(1962)**
The Man Who Shot Liberty Valence **(1962)**
The Music Man **(1962)**
Dr. No **(1962)**
Hud, **starring Paul Newman (1963)**
The Graduate, **starring Dustin Hoffman (1967)**
Bonnie and Clyde, **starring Warren Beatty and Faye Dunaway (1967)**
Guess Who's Coming to Dinner? **Starring Spencer Tracy and Katharine Hepburn (1967)**
Barefoot in the Park **(1967)**
Cool Hand Luke, **starring Paul Newman (1967)**
The Dirty Dozen **(1967)**
In Cold Blood **(1967)**
In the Heat of the Night **(1967)**
The Taming of the Shrew **(1967)**

Other notable movies of the sixties included *Psycho, Breakfast at Tiffany's, My Fair Lady, The Pink Panther, Dr. Strangelove, The Sound of Music, Doctor Zhivago, Butch Cassidy and the Sundance Kid, Rosemary's Baby, Midnight Cowboy, 2001: A Space Odyssey, The Ten Commandments, Planet of the Apes,* and *Easy Rider.*

"I'm Bond - James Bond," said secret agent 007 as he

introduced himself on the screen. Ian Fleming's British spy came to life on the big screen from his novels. With James Bond came fast cars, strange spy gadgets, and beautiful women. It all started in 1962 with *Dr. No*. Six actors portrayed Bond over a 45 year period. They included Sean Connery, George Lazenby, Roger Moore, Timothy Dalton, Pierce Brosnan, and Daniel Craig. With each actor, the James Bond character changed, from the hard and often brutal Connery hero to a more charming and soft hero. After *Dr. No* came more thrilling Bond movies all starring Sean Connery: *From Russia With Love* (1963), *Gold finger* (1964), *Thunderball* (1965), and *You Only Live Twice* (1967).

Even though we now had television in our homes, we were still drawn to the movie theaters to see all the great stars in the newest movies, such as John Wayne, Elizabeth Taylor, Richard Burton, Paul Newman, Elvis Presley, Julie Andrews, Doris Day, Rock Hudson, and Charlton Heston. Watching movies has always been a great American pastime. Summer fun was watching a movie on a giant screen at the outdoor theater. We brought our own snacks and drinks with us instead of buying them in the theater lounge snack bar. Some of us sat on lounge chairs or blankets in front of the car to watch the outdoor movie. You needed to bring some bug spray though and a flashlight to use to go to the restroom.

The Milwaukee Braves began to decline in wins and popularity. They moved from first and second place wins to fifth and sixth. The Braves moved to Atlanta in 1965 as the only major league team in the region. Milwaukee lost major league baseball for five years.

Many more songs became popular hits in the sixties. Recording artists created songs in rock, the blues, and folk music. Notables were The Beatles, The Dave Clark Five, The Rolling Stones, The Grateful Dead, Jefferson Airplane, Janis Joplin, The Mamas and the Papas, and Joan Baez. The Beatles started guest performances in America in 1964.

The A-side and the B-side intrigued song fans.

Recording artists gave us two hits for the price of one. Especially Elvis Presley, the Beatles, Rick Nelson, the Beach Boys, Brenda Lee, the Everly Brothers, and Connie Francis became known for doing this. Most often only one side of these double-sided singles was a big hit, usually the A-side, but sometimes an artist pulled a sly one and put the big hit on the B-side. Sometimes the song on the A-side was a lousy one, but the B-side one was a winner. Connie Francis, following her dad's advice was known to have given her fans good songs on both sides of her singles.

TOP HITS OF THE SIXTIES

"A Hard Day's Night" (The Beatles)
"Okie From Muskogee" (Merle Haggard & The Strangers)
"Ode to Billie Joe" (Bobbie Gentry)
"Wichita Lineman" (Glen Campbell)
"Big Bad John" (Jimmy Dean)
"Hey Jude" (The Beatles)
"A Boy Named Sue" (Johnny Cash)
"Tip-Toe Through the Tulips With Me" (Tiny Tim)
"You've Lost That Lovin' Feeling" (Righteous Brothers)
"Ain't No Mountain High Enough" (Marvin Gaye & Tammi Terrell)
"Son Of A Preacher Man" (Dusty Springfield)
"She Loves You" (The Beatles)
"Runaround Sue" (Dion and the Belmonts)
"I Got You Babe" (Sonny and Cher)
"Harper Valley P.T.A." (Jeannie C. Riley)
"Stand By Your Man" (Tammy Wynette)
"Where Have All The Flowers Gone?" (Kingston Trio)
"The Twist" (Chubby Checker)
"Sugar Sugar" (The Archies)
"To Sir With Love" (Lulu)
"Winchester Cathedral" (New Vaudeville Band)
"Johnny B. Goode" (Chuck Berry)

"Moody River" (Pat Boone)
"Tell Laura I Love Her" (Ray Peterson)
"I Could Have Danced All Night" (*My Fair Lady*)
"Raindrops Keep Fallin' on My Head" (*Butch Cassidy and the Sundance Kid;* B.J. Thomas*)*
"Mrs. Robinson" (*The Graduate*; Simon and Garfunkel)
"Everybody's Talkin'" (*Midnight Cowboy*; Harry Nilsson)
"Born to be Wild" (*Easy Rider*; Steppenwolf)
"America" (*West Side Story*)
"Supercalifragilisticexpialidocious" (*Mary Poppins*; Julie Andrews)
"The Days of Wine and Roses" *(The Days of Wine and Roses;* Frank Sinatra*)*
"Goldfinger" *(*James Bond' *Goldfinger;* Shirley Bassey*)*

    Television programs of the fifties continued to be popular, plus some new ones came on the scene.

    Sheriff Andy Taylor, a gunless lawman in the imaginary town of Mayberry, N.C., and Deputy Barney Fife came to life on the screen. Andy Griffith played the character of the sheriff and Don Knotts the deputy in the show called "The Andy Griffith Show," a show of love and laughter.

    Hanna-Barbera (Joe Barbera and Bill Hanna) created beloved cartoon characters in the TV comedies of "The Flintstones," "The Jetsons," "Yogi Bear," "Scooby-Doo," and "Huckleberry Hound."

    Jerry of "Tom and Jerry" did a classic dance scene with Gene Kelly in "Anchors Aweigh."

    A new science fiction TV series debuted in 1966, three years after JFK's assassination and ended three years later when America's Apollo 11 space shuttle landed on the moon. It was "Star Trek: The Original Series." Creator Gene Roddenberry looked on it as an outer space western. The stories appealed to the viewers' imaginations. It tells the tale of a starship's crew with a mission "to boldly go where no man has gone before." The show starred William Shatner as

Captain James Kirk, Leonard Nimoy as Spock, DeForest Kelley as Dr. Leonard "Bones" McCoy, and James Doohan as Montgomery "Scotty" Scott. "Beam me up, Scotty," shouted Capt. Kirk, as he needed to remove himself from a difficult, dangerous situation. The huge starship spacecraft the U.S.S. Enterprise being unable to land on most terrains beamed them down. It was the new frontier, the final frontier. This original series was only the beginning in science fiction entertainment. It was followed by five more TV series and 11 feature films. "Star Trek: The Next Generation" (1987-1994) received the highest ratings of any of the series, and it featured a new starship, the Enterprise-D, and a new crew 100 years later.

TELEVISION SHOWS AND PERSONALITIES OF THE SIXTIES

Jack Paar (1957-1962)
Johnny Carson (1962-1992)
"The Andy Griffith Show," **starring Andy Griffith and Don Knotts**
Dick Cavett, writing jokes for Johnny Carson, Jerry Lewis, Merv Griffin
"The Fugitive," **starring David Jannson (1963-1967)**
"The Dating Game"
"Let's Make a Deal"
"General Hospital"
"The Beverly Hillbillies"
"Petticoat Junction"
"Green Acres"
"Death Valley Days," **hosted by Ronald Reagan**
"Bewitched"
"I Dream of Jeannie"
"Fight of the Week" **(boxing)**
"All-Star Wrestling"
"The Three Stoogies" **(Larry, Curly, and Moe)**
"Days of Our Lives"

Mutual of Omaha's *"Wild Kingdom"*
"CBS Evening News," anchored by Walter Cronkite
Phyllis Diller
Kate Smith
"The George Burns and Gracie Allen Show"
Johnny Cash
"Star Trek: The Original Series" (1963-1969)

    Ronald Reagan switched to the Republican Party in 1962 and was elected Governor of California in 1966 and 1970. Reagan hosted the TV show "Death Valley Days" from 1962 to 1965.

    Walter Cronkite anchored the "CBS Evening News" for a couple decades. He interpreted for the American people such major events as the Cuban Missile Crisis, the Vietnamese War, the Apollo 11 moon landing, and the assassination of President John F. Kennedy. He covered all the wars. The moon landing was his greatest story.

    The Shiocton Union Free High School and the rural schools ended in 1961 with the formation of a K-12 district and one board of education. The high school and elementary school became one under the name of the Shiocton Joint #2 School District. Space needs being realized, a school renovation program was completed in 1962-1963, with 16 elementary classrooms, a school lunch kitchen, music room, storage rooms, a gymnasium-auditorium, showers rooms, and a new heating plant at a cost of $641,000. Ervin Colwitz, John Leitner, Ervin Moede, and Russell Omholt served the school as custodians. The school staff also included six cooks, seven contract bus owners, and four bus drivers. After a fire in 1961, the old gym was remodeled and changed into a dining hall. A referendum passed in 1969 to improve the high school facilities with a $610,000 addition to the high school.

    In 1965 the Shiocton School Board reviewed the novel *To Kill a Mockingbird* regarding questionable phrases in the book but reinstated it as required reading for high school students.

How much did things cost in the sixties? By 1960, a new house cost $12,700; a gallon of gas, 25 cents; a new car, $2,600 (a Volkswagen Beetle, $1,769; a Ford Mustang two-door hardtop, $2,368); men's Oxford shoes, $12.95; an automatic can opener, $8.88; an electric blanket, $9.94; two dozen oranges, 89 cents; a turkey ready-to-bake, 39 cents per pound; a Walnut bookcase, $29.97; a ton of coal, $14.95; and the average annual income amounted to $5,315. By 1969, a new house cost $15,500; the annual average income increased to $8,540; a gallon of gas cost 35 cents; a new car, $3.270.

Women adorned themselves with mini skirts ending well above the knee and leather boots. Men wore Paisley shirts, velvet trousers, and Oxford shoes. During the latter part of the decade men and women identified with the hippie movement. Psychedelic clothes with bright colors made the scene. Men let their hair grow longer, and women adorned themselves with longer, ankle-length skirts and dresses called maxis.

Helen Keller died in 1968. The Helen Keller-Anne Sullivan story remains one of the most interesting, exciting, and uplifting stories of mankind, a story of dedication and survival of severe handicaps.

The sixties-- a time of agitation, of ruffling the feathers, of frenziness, of steaming things up, but also of elation, of being pepped up, excited, spirited up, vitalized.

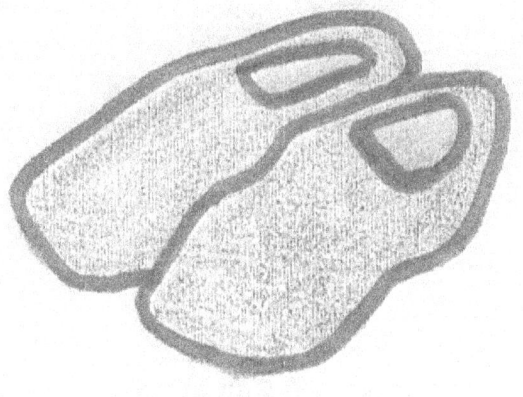

DVS 2008

OKTOBERFEST

I Am Dutch, I Am German

I am an inhabitant of the United States and have Dutch ancestors. I am likewise called a Dutch American and have lived most of my life in the State of Wisconsin.

How did this all come to pass? How did people like myself of Dutch descent come to be living in the State of Wisconsin in the United States of America? The answer is it happened through the great Dutch migration.

Colonists from the Netherlands first arrived on the eastern shores of America in 1614 and set up a town called New Amsterdam, also known as the New Netherland. It later became New York.

Two hundred Dutch men and women set up a colony in 1683 as followers of the Dutch American William Penn. German immigrants took over the colony at the beginning of the eighteenth century, and it came to be known as Germantown.

Indian tribes raided the Dutch settlements because the Indians realized the Dutch were not just visitors but taking over their land.

The Phoenix was one of the best known Dutch immigration ships. Most of the passengers died in the ship's 1847 fire near their destination.

Three other well-known Dutch immigration ships included: the Groote Beer, the Waterman, and the Zuiderkruis.

The time of travel across the Atlantic Ocean took approximately 10 days.

Immigrants came to America to obtain religious or political freedom, economic opportunity, or begin a new life in the New World.

Dutch immigration to the United States didn't have much impetus until the nineteenth century. Approximately 340,000 Dutch people settled in the United States from 1820 to 1900. The Dutch moved into Wisconsin in large numbers from 1840 to 1890. The immigrants came from southern Gelderland and North (Noord) Brabant. They came in two groups, divided by religion, Protestants and Catholics. The Protestants arrived in Wisconsin first and settled in Sheboygan County (mostly in Oostburg), Fond du Lac County, Columbia County, and La Crosse County. The Fox River Valley attracted the Catholics.

The Protestants migrated in 1844, seeking religious freedom from the Reformed Church of the Netherlands. Out of this first group came the community of Alto, established in 1845 as one of the first Dutch communities in the Midwestern United States. Not many Dutch settled in Milwaukee because they preferred to farm the lands further west.

In 1848 Father Theodore Johannes Van den Broek promoted the Dutch immigration of Catholics to Wisconsin. He helped bring over 40,000 Dutch Catholics. Most of them ended up in Green Bay and decided to stay. Some settled in at De Pere.

My ancestors had come on the scene. The Geurts and Ver Straten families emigrated to De Pere from North (Noord) Brabant, Holland in the 1870s. Grandpa Len Ver Straten and Grandma Minnie Geurts married in 1896.

After farming in De Pere for two years, Grandpa Len grew weary of the stone-filled, hilly farmland in rural De Pere and moved to Shiocton, Wisconsin. His brother Hank also moved to Shiocton, whereas their brother George and sister Annie stayed in Brown County.

Many Dutch Catholics moved into the region of the La Petite Chute community and developed farming communities in the outlying areas. Other Europeans, chiefly French and Irish emigrants, had already settled in at La Petite Chute, hence the name. La Petite Chute (Little Falls) is French. The name refers to the rapids on the Fox River. Father Theodore Van den Broek promoted Dutch immigration in this area. The town was founded as the mission of St. John Nepomucene in 1836. Families and friends moved from the Netherlands to be with family and friends in La Petite Chute. Father Van den Broek had purchased land to sell to the Dutch settlers. All of the land though wasn't farmable. Instead of plowed fields, the settlers found acres of trees. This caused the Dutch emigrants to draw straws with the winners picking the best lots. The Dutch settlers used all their time clearing land, planting, building, making fences, and raising livestock.

La Petite Chute, upon petition by the residents, became incorporated as the Village of Little Chute in 1899.

At least 40,000 Dutch Catholics immigrated to the Little Chute area by 1927. Little Chute became the largest Dutch Catholic community in the United States.

Some Dutch immigrant families didn't like the land Father Van den Broek was selling at La Petite Chute, and they bought land farther east. They called their new settlement Franciscan Bosh, but it was more commonly known as the Village of Holland or Hollandtown. Hollandtown is located on County Trunk D from Kaukauna and listed on maps as Holland.

A popular place in Hollandtown is Van Abel's, a family owned and operated restaurant with a banquet hall for special events. I've enjoyed some delicious meals there and gone to wedding receptions and dances there, too.

The Dutch influence on America is well-known. The Dutch supplied arms to the Thirteen Colonies during the American War of Independence. The American flag was first saluted by the Dutch. Three American Presidents had Dutch surnames: Martin van Buren, Theodore Roosevelt, and Franklin D. Roosevelt. Van Buren spoke Dutch.

Dutch was spoken in Little Chute up to the twentieth century. Dutch newspapers were published in De Pere by Catholic clergymen up to the time of World War I.

Famous Dutch Americans included Willem de Kooning in art, Piet Mondriaan in art, Janwillem van de Wetering in detective fiction, Edward W. Bok (a Pulitzer Prize winner and creator of the word "living room"), Eddie van Halen in music, and Peter Stuyvesant in politics.

The most famous Dutch painter was Rembrandt Harmenszoon van Rijn. Other Dutch painters included Johannes Vermeer, Frans Hals, Vincent van Gogh, and Piet Mondriaan.

The Dutch festival of Sinterklaas was celebrated as St. Nick's Day (December 5) until the late 1960's in Little Chute. The Dutch festival of Kermis has been celebrated in Little Chute since 1981.

The "schut" celebration, a centuries old rifle competition, occurs each fall. There is no competition like it in this country. It got its start in the Netherlands after the Crusades. The "schut" was first held in 1850 in Hollandtown and has been held every year since.

The Dutch are proud of their heritage, but they gave up windmills and canals in favor of modern industry to do better dairy farming and cheese processing.

Over five million persons of Dutch heritage live in present-day America. Most live in New York, California, Michigan, Iowa, Pennsylvania, and Wisconsin.

Besides being Dutch, I am also German. My siblings

and I are mostly Dutch, but we have some German in us, too. I think the German comes from my mother, Cecilia Fern Dietzler, and her side of the family. Ma said we had some Swiss and Indian in us, too.

German Americans account for the largest ancestral group in America, approximately 49 million. The largest populations of Germans exist in California and Texas, although the Midwestern States of North Dakota and Wisconsin boast the higher proportions.

The first Germans coming to America settled in Jamestown, Virginia in 1608. Huge numbers of Germans, however, didn't arrive until the 1680s, occupying New York and Pennsylvania. The number of German immigrations was the highest from 1840 to 1900, approximately eight million.

The influence of German immigrants is seen in our American cuisine. Frankfurters (also known as wieners), hamburgers, bratwurst, sauerkraut, and strudel have German origin. The pretzel came from German bakers.

The Germans overtook the beer industry after 1850. The Anheuser-Busch Company was created by German immigrants Eberhard Anheuser and Adolphus Busch in 1860.

The German-American celebrations of Oktoberfest and Von Steuben Day occur regularly in America. German Fest is celebrated annually in Milwaukee.

American Presidents of German descent include: Dwight Eisenhower (Eisenhauer), Herbert Hoover (Huber), Richard Milhous Nixon (Melhausen), George W. Bush, George H.W. Bush, and Theodore Roosevelt.

Thus, Dear Reader, much of our heritage and customs in the United States, including the Midwestern State of Wisconsin, come from the Dutch and the Germans.

The De Groots

Ver Straten Twins

I always thought there were no twins on the Van Straten side of the family, but my thinking was faulty. There were twins indeed in the Van Straten ancestry.

Great-grandpa Martin and his brother Peter Johannes "John" were twins, both born minutes apart on July 25, 1836, in North (Noord) Brabant, Holland.

Martin's and John's parents were Gerardus "George" and Adianna Dehlia "Delia" (Kuypers) Ver Straten. They lived in North (Noord) Brabant, Holland when Martin and John were born. Eight children were born to George and Delia. Not much is known of their children, except for Martin, John, and Petronella. The names of four of the other children were Hendrina, Maria, Henrikus, and Marianna.

Petronella was born in Zeeland, Holland on March 12, 1847.

John married Anna Van Den in 1860, and they had nine children named Mary, John, Peter, Delia, Martin, George, Henry, Ellen, and Nellie. Nellie died in infancy and John at the age of 12. Mary married Frank De Cleene. Peter married Frank's sister, Louise De Cleene. Delia married Phil Dhoogs.

Martin married Anna Van Vonderen. George married Hacker, with a second marriage to Sarah. Henry married Christine Van Vonderen, Anna's sister. Ellen married Jake Vande Hei.

Great-grandpa Martin married Gertrude Van Der Wise in 1870. They had six children. Two died as infants. The names of the others were George, Leonard, Annie, and Henry "Hank."

George married Gertrude, and they had four children named Gertrude, Martha, Rose Mary, and Peter.

Annie married Bat Gleason. Their son Ray married Hanna Voss, and they had four children named Betty, Ray, Bat, and Marion.

Henry "Hank" married Rose Dollar, and they had 10 children named Catherine, Irene, Harold, Frances "Tootie," Helen, Lloyd, Dale, Raymond, Margaret, and Roy.

Grandpa Leonard married Wilhelmina Johanna Guerts in 1896, and they had 14 children named Anna, Francis "Sis," Martha, Aloysius, Henry, Grace, Glen, Marie, Agnes "Dolly," Rosa "Hootsie" "Sister Lurana Marie," Robert "Bob," Clark, Carmen, and Erna.

Gertrude died in 1882, and Martin married Katrina Burke Smit in 1885.

Coming to America

John Ver Straten, son of George and Delia, came to the United States in 1865 to decide if he found living here acceptable. He soon discovered he liked it and convinced Martin to come. Martin took leave of his home and friends in the spring of 1866, accompanied by Anna Van Den, John's fiancée, and probably also his sister Petronella. They traveled via Dutch immigration ship from Rotterdam, Holland to Hull, England and to Liverpool, England. Travel from there was on a vessel bound for New York and from there they traveled to Little Chute, Wisconsin (known then as La Petite Chute).

Martin and John later moved to De Pere, Wisconsin.

They purchased 40 acres of partly cleared land in partnership, living in a small log house.

Martin returned to Holland in the fall of 1869 and married Gertrude Van Der Wise in the spring of 1870. After getting married Martin and Gertrude sailed from Rotterdam, Holland to Portland, Maine. They took the Grand Funk Railroad to Chicago, Illinois to De Pere, Wisconsin.

Petronella's Family

Petronella moved to the Green Bay region, met Henry De Groot, and they married in 1868. They had four boys and two girls named Bernard, George, John Antone, Cornelius, Dehlia, and Gertrude.

John Antone, known as a tall, rugged man with a fearless nature, had the ambition to be a farmer, as was the tradition of many Dutch settlers. His brother Bernard "Barney" had moved onto a farm in Wausaukee, and John Antone went to work on the farm and met the beautiful Justine De Bot and married her in 1904. They obtained a farm northeast of Wausaukee known as the Bill Wartick farm but in 1917 moved to a farm southeast of Wausaukee.

John and Justine, like many families of this time period, had a large family of nine boys and three girls named Edwin Henry, Raymond Victor, Eunice Veronica, Gerald John, Harold Louis, Cyril Alphonse, Mary Elizabeth, Randall Damian, Rita Catherine, John Joseph, Richard Paul, and Robert Anthony.

John Antone was a hard-working man and a good manager. When his boys grew big enough to do the farm work, John went on the road working jobs, like repairing roads, logging, and any odd job, as he was good at doing anything.

John's boys didn't become farmers but took up the trades of mechanics, electricians, or carpenters, all excellent tradesmen. The farm probably lost its appeal because of rock picking or cleaning the barn.

The smoke house burned down once, and it was full of meat.

The farm had a lovers lane, a discontinued roadway at the edge of the farm, and it was used by quite a few.

Every farm boy and girl had to take turns with pumping the cream separator. They had to help make butter, too.

Washing was done on a wash board until all the children were grown.

A case of scarlet fever surfaced in 1925, and everyone had to be quarantined. Part of the family stayed in the milk house and barn and the sick ones in the house.

John sold the farm in 1945. John was a strong man even as he got older, doing hard work after the age of 80. He died at the age of 92, having lived a hard and useful life.

MEMORIES

*I remember taking the motor vehicle road test three times
       before passing.
I remember applying for a Social Security card.
I remember working in a canning plant.
I remember working at the Hortonville Toy Factory.
I remember going to the fair and the circus.*

The Summer of '57

Making Money for College

During my first two years of college I expected costs to be minimal. I only needed money for spending and incidental expenses, like pencils, ink, tablets, and clothes. I didn't have the expense of maintaining a motor vehicle. Nonetheless, I did need a summer job.

I needed to get my drivers license before I started a summer job. During the waiting time, I earned some money picking beans at Lloyd's or cucumbers for Anthony's. I did anything to earn money to add to my college savings.

Pa took me out driving a few times to show me how to do what was required on the driving road test. It was important to know how to park on a hill, to turn around on a road, and to parallel park.

Pa drove me to New London to take the tests. I passed the written test with flying colors, but I didn't do well on the actual driving test. The first time the lights or signals on Pa's car didn't pass inspection. After those defects were fixed, we made our second trip to New London, and I goofed up by driving through a stop sign. It took a third time for me to finally pass the road test and get my license.

The Hortonville Canning Company was hiring. I applied and got hired. Since it was my first job, I had to fill out an application for a Social Security card.

When I started working at the canning company, they were canning peas, beans, and corn. The work being done was exciting to watch. I watched the workers on the line filling the cans with vegetables and putting them in boxes. Once enough boxes had been filled and fastened, my work began. I loaded the boxes of canned peas, corn, and beans onto a cart. After enough carts were loaded, I stacked the boxes in the warehouse for shipping.

My job at the canning company lasted only a few weeks. I went back to picking beans and cukes until I got another job.

Pa talked to his friend Russell Johnson about getting me a job at the Hortonville Toy Factory. I did get hired and worked at the Toy Factory the rest of the summer. The work at the Toy Factory satisfied me. I sanded pieces of wood destined to become part of a toy for some lucky little boy or girl.

I helped out with the work on the farm whenever I wasn't working and even if I was working I helped out on weekends.

I earned $257 in 1957 in Hortonville at the Canning Company and the Toy Factory.

Summertime Fun

We always found time for fun. We went to the movies. We picnicked. We went swimming at Dyne's Swimming Hole and under the Shiocton bridge. Most everyone went dancing on Saturday nights. We went to weddings, one after another.

Going to the homecomings and the Outagamie County Fair at Seymour was a big attraction for all of us. Once school was out, all we talked about was going to the county fair at Seymour and the homecomings at Shiocton, Black Creek, and

Hortonville. We talked about what we wanted to do and see at those events.

The homecoming parades were exhilarating. What made it so exciting was watching the marching bands, the colorful floats, and friends and relatives performing in the parades.

The amusement rides at the homecomings were most often provided by Tip Top Shows, a Waupaca firm operating rides at about 30 events each year from April to September. The Tip Top Shows also provided rides at the county fairs at Seymour, Shawano, Oshkosh, Plymouth, and many other places..

We had loads of fun riding the Merry-Go-Round, the Ferris Wheel, the Tilt-a-Whirl, the swings, the Octopus, playing the midway games, including throwing balls at targets, throwing darts at balloons, shooting corks at targets, and playing the game wheel. We danced to rock and roll tunes in the pavilion or hall and ate cotton candy and Carmel Corn.

The county fair offered even more than the homecomings, including: big, warm toasted pretzels, popcorn, ice cream, and sweet corn; free pencils, rulers, and balloons in the exhibit halls; the sideshows on the midway, featuring the bearded lady, giant steers, midgets, the haunted house, and the carnival; tractor pulls, horse pulls, and shows in the grandstand, and the barn buildings filled with cows, horses, pigs, chickens, rabbits, and so forth.

The state fair thrilled us even more, with cream puffs, dairy shows, ice skating shows, livestock judging, and the grandstand shows.

The Barnum and Bailey Circus made a regular appearance in the summer, with the elephants, wild cats, aerialists, magicians, and clowns shows in the three rings. Buying some peanuts, popcorn, or Carmel corn to eat during the shows made it even more enjoyable.

Thus ends the summer of '57, a summer of work, adventure, and fun.

OSC

Oshkosh State College (OSC) started out as a Normal School in 1871, a three-story building with 18 rooms to use for classrooms and offices. The building cost $70,000. George Sumner Albee became the first president of the school. Six teachers taught 43 students. By the time I attended college at OSC 90 years later, approximately135 teachers taught 2,200 students in 11 huge buildings.

Under President Albee additions were added to the original Normal School building, and a gym was built. The gym never had a name. Students and teachers called it the Gym or the Old Gym.

Rufus Henry Halsey came to the school in 1898. Social activities blossomed on campus under President Halsey, and he succeeded in getting a science building constructed.

The campus expanded markedly under President John Alexander Hull Keith. He arrived in 1907, and the Old Gym became the second largest gymnasium in the State of Wisconsin and one of the best-equipped.

In 1916 a fire destroyed all the buildings on campus except for the Old Gym. Classes had to be held in the local churches and the high school building.

In1917 the school name changed from Oshkosh

Normal School to Oshkosh State Teachers College under the direction of President Harry Alvin Brown. The college became one of the first ten teachers colleges to be members of the North Central Association. President Brown succeeded in completing the construction of an administration building in honor of Edward Joseph Dempsey, longtime President of the Board of Regents, and a training school in honor of Rose C. Swart, as well as an athletic field.

Forrest R. Polk

Forrest Raymond Polk came to the college in 1931 and was still there during my first two years of college at OSC. President Polk added more required subjects and stronger majors and minors. A Liberal Arts curriculum was added, and the name of the college changed from Oshkosh State Teachers College to Wisconsin State College at Oshkosh. Some residence halls or dormitories became a reality under the direction of President Polk, all for women-- Pollock House, Radford Hall, and Webster Hall.

Albee Hall, built in 1954, housed one large and one small gymnasium, a swimming pool, offices, and locker rooms. It was named in honor of the first president of the college.

A student union, Reeve Memorial Union, also came on the scene at the OSC campus in 1959, providing a meeting place for students.

When I started college in 1957, no men's residence halls or dormitories existed on the Oshkosh campus. The first men's residence hall, Clemans Hall, opened in 1960, named in honor of a former physics instructor, Dean of Men, and Vice-President of the college.

No fraternity house existed until 1960 when the Lyceum Fraternity acquired their own house.

The Old Gym was demolished in 1962, and a new library was built in its place. The library provided much needed space for more books and reference materials, study rooms, and workrooms.

Roger Guiles

President Roger Guiles came to the college in 1959. He was an active and encouraging president, meeting the challenges of a growing student body.

Private housing dominated the OSC scene-- off

campus private housing. Most students rented a room or an apartment, although apartments cost more. They cooked at their residence or ate out. Most of the housing existed within a short walking distance from campus. All male students lived off campus. Many female students lived off campus also, although the campus included two women's residence halls, namely Pollock House and Radford Hall. All off campus housing, however, had to meet approval when students registered.

Campus social life attracted and excited the OSC student. A Social Life Committee of 15 students sponsored many activities on campus, including the Homecoming, the Prom, the Thanksgiving and Christmas Formals, all-school mixer dances, and the Sunday night movies. Many other campus activities occurred, including Honors Day, the Mother's Day Tea, Iota Fraternity's Songfest, sororities and fraternities, Student Council, Vet's Club, choir, band, forensics, drama, Language Club, International Relations Club, the Advance and Quiver, religious societies (Inter-Faith Council, Wesley, Newman Club), Ugly Man and Sweetheart contests, campus carnival, athletics (football, basketball, track, golf, tennis), cheerleading, synchronized swimming, modern dance, ice carving contests, and ice skating. Off campus activities included roller skating, the movies, and dancing at the Rail Bar. I often went ice skating and played ice hockey on weekends at home in Shiocton.

The students were supported by their professors in all campus life activities. A professor became involved with each group or club, participating in the events of each.

Early morning classes, meeting friends in the cafeteria, spending hours in the library, joining clubs, cheering at the big games, and taking tests rounded out our social life. The academic halls became part of our lives. Rushing became a part of our lives-- rushing to and from classes. We always had to take time to read the black board and postings in Dempsey Hall. It was our life. We were the Titans.

MEMORIES

*I remember many Shiocton High School graduates
    attending college.
I remember many of my cousins attending college.
I remember catching rides to Oshkosh with Bill Steede.
I remember living at Mrs. Brahe's private boarding home.
I remember working in the kitchen and dining room at Mrs.
    Brahe's home.*

Getting My Feet Wet

I was anxious to attend college at OSC. I had my sights set on becoming a teacher. I chose to go to Oshkosh State College because everyone else from Shiocton was going there and it was close to home and affordable. The major expense of housing didn't matter to me because I had an opportunity to earn my room and board at an off campus boarding home.

Many more high school graduates started attending college, including Shiocton High School graduates. Some jobs or occupations required a college degree. College enrollments increased. Registrations at OSC went over 2,000 during the mid-nineteen fifties.

Jackie and Jane Van Straten each attended schools of nursing and became nurses. Jackie studied x-ray technology at Mercy Hospital, Oshkosh, and worked as an x-ray technician at the Community Hospital, New London, and the Theda Clark Hospital, Neenah, later working in nuclear medicine at St. Mary's Hospital, Green Bay. Jane studied x-ray technology at the Theda Clark Hospital's School of X-Ray Technology and worked as an x-ray technician at Theda Clark, later becoming a manager in the radiology department. Jackie and Jane are progeny of Uncle Clark and Aunt Nona.

Besides my brother Russell and myself, others attending college at OSC included Bill Steede, David Reinke,

Sally, Sandra, and Bob Joe Brownson, Bill Herminath, Pat Kennedy, Sue Andrews, James Countney, and C.J. Van Patten. Sally, Sandra, and Bob Joe are progeny of Aunt Dolly and Uncle Clarence.

Occasionally, I crossed paths with my cousin Larry Lucht from Manawa, studying in OSC's Reserve Library. Patsy Lucht entered the Sisterhood, taking on the new name of Sister Lisa. Larry and Patsy are progeny of Aunt Carmen and Uncle Bill.

Bill Herminath attended OSC for two years (1957-1958 and 1958-1959) and worked for Uncle Sam for two years. He married Doris Surprise and worked at Appleton Papers of Appleton as a materials control technician.

Cousin Bob Brownson attended OSC during the 1959-1960 college year, followed by employment with the Sommers Construction firm in Shiocton, later becoming a foreman with the firm. He married Nancy Kable.

Margo Bergstresser attended college and became a teacher.

Bill Bergstresser and Mark Brownson (progeny of Aunt Dolly and Uncle Clarence) attended the Outagamie County Teachers College at Kaukauna.

Some Shiocton High School graduates, particularly Jerry Ratsch, attended the University of Wisconsin at Madison, WI. Russell went there to do his graduate studies, earning his Masters Degree in Education.

Darla Close, Mary Ort, and Delores McHugh also attended college. Darla Close became a registered nurse. Barbara Allen became a beautician. Nelson Greely studied engineering at the Appleton Vocational School. Delores McHugh became a home economics teacher in the Shiocton School District. Mary Ort became a nursing instructor and married a doctor. Patricia Ritchie became a beautician and JoAnn Theede an x-ray technician. Norita Van Straten (progeny of my godparent's Dale and Phyllis) learned to be a nursing assistant and worked at the New London Community

Hospital. Patricia Wolf attended the Appleton School of Business.

We all seemed to be following Our Class Motto: "Our Aim, Success; Our Hope, To Win."

My cousin Dorothy Mae graduated from OSC, when it was called Oshkosh State Teachers College, with a Bachelor of Science degree in Education. She taught school for five years, two in Sheboygan and three in Green Bay. After marrying Fred "Fritz" Christman in 1950, Dorothy Mae became a stay-at-home mom. Dorothy Mae is progeny of Uncle Henry and Aunt Agnes.

My cousins of Uncle Bob's and Aunt Dorothy's family studied and entered the nursing field. Rose Ann graduated from St. Agnes Hospital's School of Radiology and became a registered technologist. Julie Ann graduated from Fox Valley Technical College, becoming a licensed practical nurse. Bridget Ann and Peter became registered nurses, Bridget graduating from the Mercy Medical Center's School of Nursing and Peter from Eau Claire Technical College. Catherine Ann became a certified nursing assistant.

All my cousins from Uncle Glen's and Aunt Carolyn's family graduated from college. Jim graduated from St. Norbert's, served in the U.S. Army, earned many sports awards and a Masters Degree in Education and a Ph.D. in educational administration. Joan, Donna, Bonnie, Patsy, and Marie graduated from the University of Wisconsin at Madison, all affiliated with the teaching profession. Joan earned a Masters in educational psychology. Donna taught speech and English. Donna and Joan are published authors. Bonnie worked in speech therapy. Patsy became a reading specialist and earned a Masters in Reading. Marie became an elementary teacher. Terry, also a teacher, earned a Masters in special education.

My cousin Cynthia (Sommers) Trettin of the Carol and Eddie Sommers family became a teacher at the Milton Hershey School in Pennsylvania and also became a registered nurse. Carol is progeny of Aunt Grace and Uncle Mike.

Many high school graduates from Shiocton not attending college were just as smart as those attending college.

Being a college graduate didn't guarantee a higher wage. A person without a college degree was able to bring home just as big a paycheck.

Jack Andrews became a Chevrolet dealer at Sielaff-Andrews of Shiocton, following in his father Don's footsteps.

Mary Ellen Sykes married Gil Knoke and worked as a cook in the Shiocton School District.

Cousin Mike became the owner of Van Straten Construction of Shiocton.

Cousin Tom managed the Terra fertilizer business.

Joe Buss married my cousin Maxine Miller and worked at Kimberly-Clark in Neenah. Cousin Dick also worked at Kimberly-Clark. Carl also worked in a Neenah plant and later took charge of Frank's Kraut in Black Creek when Uncle Glen retired. Carl raised cabbage on the side on the farm and developed a reputation as an excellent manager in the cabbage production business.

I didn't own a car during my first year of college. I borrowed Pa's car whenever possible. I drove the tractor to town a few times but only during daylight hours.

We car pooled to Oshkosh. Anyone from Shiocton having wheels and attending OSC ended up with riders. Some of us rode with Bill Steede. It was common courtesy to tip the driver with some cash for gas, like $5.

In the fall of 1957 when I enrolled as a freshman, Russell was returning as a senior.

Russell lived in a boarding home during the school year. This living arrangement had been made possible through a friend from Shiocton, Ronnie Groth. Ronnie's dad, Martin Groth, had served on the Village Board for many years. Now I had a chance to live at this boarding home through Russell. Living at this home was a stroke of luck. We earned our room and board by performing light housekeeping duties.

The boarding home was owned and operated by Mrs. Mary J. Brahe. Living with and working for Mrs. Brahe was like living at home.

The boarding home was located at 261 Jackson Street. The City of Oshkosh, however, changed the house numbers during the year of 1957. The address for the boarding home, therefore, changed to 515 Jackson Street. It was located on Jackson Street between the Union Avenue and Church Avenue intersections. It was also the last residence before the Winnebago County Court House, just immediately south.

Mrs. Brahe's boarding home (1957)

Traveling from Shiocton to Mrs. Brahe's home was simple. Take State Hwy. 76 south of Shiocton all the way to Oshkosh. At the outskirts of Oshkosh, State Hwy. 76 intercepted with U.S. Hwy. 45 south, and it ran right into Jackson Street.

Mrs. Brahe housed four or five boarders and, if possible, four students. Sometimes the fifth boarder might be a boarding student paying for room and board. Besides Russell and I from Shiocton, the other two students were a sister and brother from Clintonville, Patsy and Terry Dunlavy. Patsy was a junior. Terry, a freshman, had attended the Sacred Heart Seminary in Oneida, Wisconsin for four years.

Our housekeeping duties included setting the dining table, serving the food, cleanup, and washing dishes for breakfast, lunch, and dinner seven days a week. Sometimes we helped prepare some of the food being served. We learned much about cooking and table etiquette from Mrs. Brahe. On Saturdays we vacuumed and dusted all the boarding rooms. We had the extra responsibilities of sweeping and shoveling the porch and putting away food staples delivered by the grocer. We had opportunities to rake and mow the lawn, but Mrs. Brahe paid us for doing those duties.

The front door was never locked.

Upon walking up the front steps and entering the front door, you encountered steps going upstairs, a sunroom, and a small hallway leading to the living room.

Mrs. Brahe's chair occupied a spot by the window in the living room. A TV and approximately six chairs were also located in the living room. Two boarding rooms adjoined the living room.

Next to the living room was the dining room. Mrs. Brahe's desk and chair occupied a corner of this room. A large dining table and chairs took up most of the space in the dining room. Adjoining the dining room were another boarding room, a restroom, and the kitchen. Mrs. Brahe's bedroom adjoined the kitchen and steps led to the basement, the back door, and the upper floor.

At the top of the steps to the upper floor was another boarding room to the left and a long, narrow room to the right. This long, narrow room had a skylight and a door at each end of the room. This room was used as a laundry room, restroom, and bathroom. When using this room as a restroom or bathroom, you had to walk down the whole length of the room to lock both doors. When finished, both doors had to be unlocked again. There were two more boarding rooms on the other end of the long, narrow room and steps to the downstairs and steps leading to a third level.

Patsy occupied a room at the end of the long, narrow room on the upper floor. The room had no door, but there was a room divider for privacy.

Room was available for four students, usually male, to live at this third level. It was a gutted out attic with the walls slanted, complete with four beds, lamps, dressers, and desks. Russell, Terry, and I bunked up at this level.

We had no TV upstairs, but we were welcome to watch television programs in the downstairs living room with Mrs. Brahe and the ladies.

Mrs. Brahe was a big woman. She had long hair put up into a bun. A few newspapers cushioned the chair she sat on.

I continued to be enuretic. I had to change the linens on my bed myself now. It wasn't a problem though. There were multiple linens, and the washing was easy. Mrs. Brahe had an extra washing machine and lines in the basement.

We scheduled our classes around mealtimes in order to be at Mrs. Brahe's on time to set the table, serve the food, do cleanup, and the dishes.

Mrs. Brahe let some of us go home on weekends. She wanted at least two students there on weekends to clean the boarding rooms. Sometimes only one of us went home on a weekend. Russell and I didn't always go home on the same weekend.

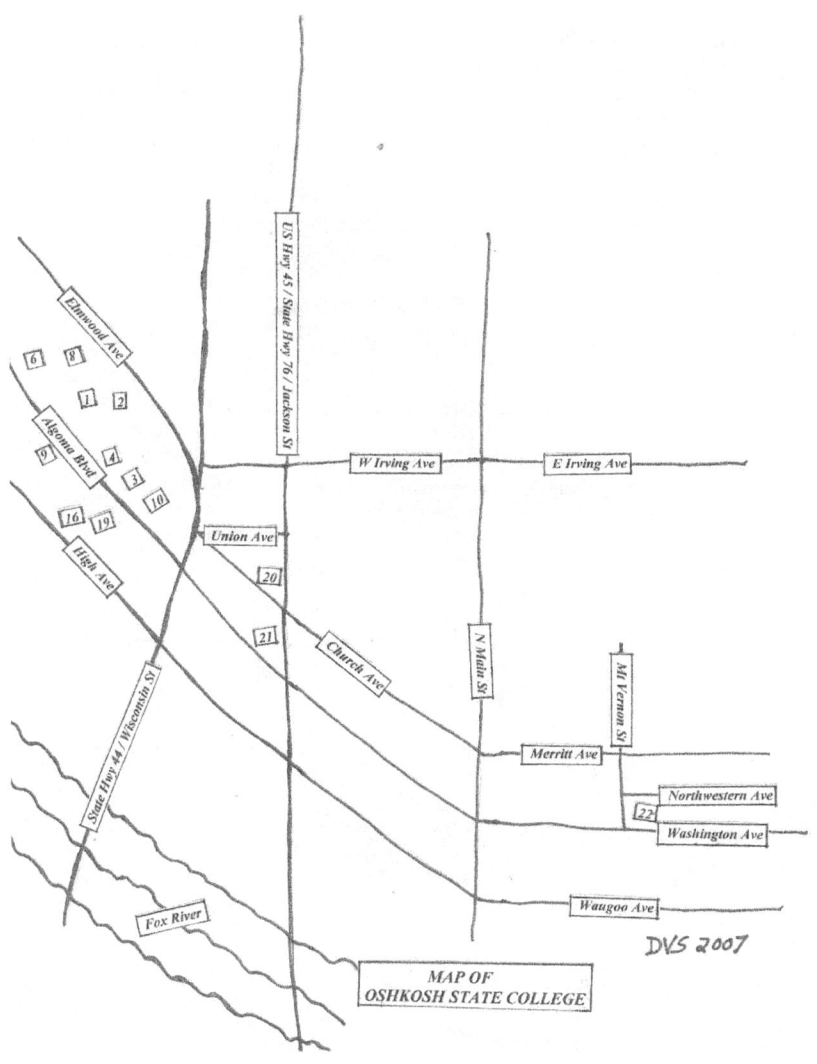

OSC CAMPUS (AND VICINITY) MAP KEY

1. Dempsey Hall (1917)
2. Old Gym (1908) / Forrest R. Polk Library (1962)
3. Reeve Memorial Union (1959)
4. Albee Hall (1954)
6. Rose C. Swart Training School (1929) / Swart Hall
8. Harrington Hall (1913)
9. Radford Hall (1951)
10. Clemans Hall (1960)
16. Webster Hall (1958)
19. Pollock House (1943)
20. Mary Brahe House (515 Jackson Street)
21. Winnebago County Court House (415 Jackson Street)
22. Oshkosh Public Library (106 Washington Avenue)

MEMORIES

I remember registering for college classes at OSC.
I remember walking to school on Algoma Boulevard.
I remember using the microscope in Botany lab.
I remember the "Spanish Fiesta" all school dance.
I remember the Latin banquet.

A Gullible Greenhorn

College classes began on September 10 for the 1957-1958 school year.

Students started arriving a week before classes commenced in order to get settled in. Everyone needed time to move their personal belongings into their off campus residences. I didn't have much to move into Mrs. Brahe's house, only my suitcase of clothes and a box of school supplies.

Russell introduced me to Mrs. Brahe. We talked some before moving our belongings to the upper level. I settled in at the middle of the room, with bed, dresser, desk, chair, and lamp. Russell located himself with similar furnishings at the south end of the room, and Terry did the same on the north end of the room. Space and furnishings were available for another student between Russell and myself.

After we finished moving in at Mrs. Brahe's, we needed to register for classes. Russell helped orient me through the registration process. Registration occurred in the gymnasium in Albee Hall. We had to go through several stations during registration. Forms needed to be filled out. We filled them out on chest-high tables. We didn't register for any class held during the lunch hour, unless it was a required class only held then. Some classes I had chosen ended up being cancelled or full. I had to keep switching until I came up with a full load of classes.

The last part of registering was getting residence approval. I was thrilled Russell was first in line during this last part of the registration process. When Russell mentioned Mrs. Brahe's boarding home as the choice for off-campus housing, he was told it wasn't on the approved residency list. This delayed the process. Russell called Mrs. Brahe and told her she wasn't on the approved list. Several minutes of calling occurred before the problem was solved. Once Russell's residency approval was complete, my time spent at this station went quick.

College students at OSC were allowed to take up to 18 credits per semester. Each student was assigned an advisor, and the advisor recommended the number of credits to take, based on the difficulty of each course. Most courses were three-credit classes, some two credits, and it was a rarity to take a one-credit class. Biology courses were five-credit classes, three credits for lecture classes and two credits for lab.

We picked up our books after registration at the rental library. There were pros and cons to renting books. It was cost effective but borrowed books often were all marked up by former users. For some courses the student, however, had to buy a book or two at the student union.

I walked to school. I headed south on Jackson Street to Algoma Boulevard and headed west on Algoma. Occasionally I walked to campus via Church Street.

I didn't overburden myself with books on my walks to school. I only carried the books I needed for my morning classes, dropped them off at noon, and took different books after lunch for my afternoon classes.

If rain was predicted or expected, I wore or took along my raincoat and a plastic bag to protect my books. Sometimes I got caught in a rainstorm. I, of course, got soaked and my books got wet.

Sometimes I needed to use the public library, the Oshkosh Public Library. To get there, I headed east on Algoma Boulevard off Jackson Street and on to Washington Avenue. It was a short distance from Mrs. Brahe's, taking only a few minutes.

Walking along campus on Algoma Boulevard, the first building on the left side was Pollock House, followed by Webster Hall (under construction until 1958) and then Radford Hall. The first building on the right side was Clemans Hall (1960), followed by the Reeve Memorial Union (1959), Albee Hall, Dempsey Hall, the Old Gym (the Forrest R. Polk Library, 1962), the Rose C. Swart Training School, and Harrington Hall.

The Reeve Memorial Union became the living room on campus. It was a coffeehouse, bookstore, pool room, dining hall, snack bar, lounge, reading room, concert hall, and meeting room, but most of all a place to go.

Albee Hall housed a gymnasium, swimming pool, lockers, and offices.

Webster Hall and Radford Hall were women's residence halls and Clemans Hall the first men's residence hall.

Dempsey Hall was the administration building, housing the administration rooms and offices, classrooms, and a second-floor library. The library in Dempsey Hall and the Old Gym ended in 1962 when the Forrest R. Polk Library was built.

Harrington Hall was used for science classes.

The Rose C. Swart Training School housed classrooms for all the grades and junior high school and was used for practice teaching.

Writing continued to be done with the fountain pen although the ballpoint pen was patented in the 1940s. The ballpoint pen contained ink in an inner chamber held back by a steel ball. Pressing on the ball put ink on the ball and onto the writing paper. Companies like Eversharp still hadn't perfected the ballpoint's steel ball. It was either too big preventing ink coming out or too small leaking out.

The fountain pen had an inner rubber chamber filled with ink. Pressing the pen's point released ink onto the wtiting paper. Writing with the fountain pen often was smudgy. An ink blotter was used to soak up the ink smudges. If the smudges became gross looking, the writer had to crumple up the paper and start over. If you ran out of ink and then refilled the pen, the writing wasn't even because the ink came out thick. Ink came out thick when refilled and thinned down when the chamber was almost empty.

Professors accepted hand written reports yet as long as they were written in ink and not in pencil. The trend, however, was moving towards typewritten reports. The Smith Corona Company offered manual typewriters for sale, and the cost became affordable to the college student. Oshkosh State College also accommodated the student by setting up a typewriter pool. About a dozen typewriters were available for use as long as the college doors were open, usually from 6:00 a.m. until 10:00 p.m. daily.

Practical Arts 6 (Typing), a credited, ungraded class, was offered during my first semester, and I enrolled in it. Ruth

Ruth Nelson

Nelson, the Dean of Women, taught the class. Mrs. Nelson was one the best faculty members and one of my favorite teachers. I improved my typing skills under her tutelage. I began using the typewriter pool to type my class reports. The professors appreciated the typed report, and a better grade was deemed possible with one.

Russell   **Bill Steede**

Russell and Bill Steede were finishing up their studies at OSC, taking final classes to complete their majors and education requirements. They both graduated with B.S. Degrees. Russell graduated with a Biology major and minors in English and History, whereas Bill earned a Math major and a Biology minor.

Terry Dunlavy, our roommate, once remarked, "Russell hardly studies or opens a book but gets excellent grades, whereas we are studying hard all the time to make the grade."

Russell taught school in Auburndale and Winneconne. Actually, after obtaining a Masters Degree from the University of Wisconsin, Madison, Russell became a guidance counselor. When the position became available, Russell took on the job of registrar at Fox Valley Tech in Appleton. Russell married Geraldine "Gerri" Williamson in 1960, and they had four children (Jeff, Laurie, Stephanie, and Andy) and 10 grandchildren.

Botany, also known as phytology, is the study of plants. The OSC frosh studied botany all year in the Biology 10a and Biology 10b courses, five credits per semester. We studied algae and fungi, plant structures, development, and diseases. Much of our class time was devoted to the study of cells, their structure and content.

Daniel Palm

Dr. Daniel Palm taught botany. He knew everything about plants. His classroom was like a small auditorium with rows of seats escalating upwards. Dr. Palm wrote everything he said in lecture on the blackboard. He used two boards, filling both boards as he moved along in his lecture. As the boards filled up with his writing, he erased the previous one in order to keep proceeding with his writing.

Biology courses were assigned five credits because a portion of the course was devoted to lab work. The course consisted of three lecture class hours and two lab hours per week.

Botany lab work exhilarated me. We used the microscope. We put slides of liquid or solid samples from a culture under the microscope. Some slides were already made up, and some we had to make up ourselves. We needed to make drawings of what we viewed under the microscope-- amoeba, algae, cells, and so forth. I thoroughly enjoyed making these drawings. I created colored drawings and received excellent grades on them.

In addition to botany, my course load for each semester of my freshman year included: English 1a and 1b (English Composition), three credits per semester; Geography 1 (World Geography), three credits; Geography 6 (Climates and Weather Patterns), three credits; History 6a and 6b (Early and Modern Civilization), four credits per semester; and, Physical Education 13 and 14 (Physical Training and Exercise), one credit per semester. I had a course load of 16 credits per semester during my freshman year at OSC. Since each credit equaled one hour of class time, I had 16 hours of class time per week.

Bill Safranek   **William Thompson**

Professor Bill Safranek taught Enghish composition. He drilled us on English grammar, and we had to write several essays and a term paper each semester.

Dr. William Thompson lectured us on early and modern history. He shared many facts and dates. I think he was a little over my head-- I mean I don't know if I understood everything he was telling us. Remembering all the facts and dates was difficult. Dr. Thompson had written a book and had it published during my freshman year at OSC. His book was entitled *The Image of War*.

Kuei-Sheng Chang   **Warner Geiger**

Professors Kuei-Sheng Chang and Warner Geiger taught us geography. I learned some interesting facts in their classes, but geography wasn't my best subject. Just imagine-- I actually had a Chinese professor.

Robert Kolf   **Eric Kitzman**

I didn't get out of Phy. Ed. Class yet. All frosh had to take physical education class both semesters. Dr. Robert Kolf and his assist Eric Kitzman kept us in tip-top shape.

Our professors accommodated us in getting our semester grade results fast. We gave them a self-addressed stamped envelope, and they mailed our grades to us.

I just managed to pass Geography. I got a C grade in History-- this was an achievement for me. I received B's in Phy. Ed., English, and Botany. I achieved a grade point high enough to allow me to continue on with my sophomore year at OSC.

Campus Spotlight

OSC students enjoyed the school year through many social and campus life events and activities. Marilyn

Marilyn Schroeder

Schroeder was the most popular student on campus, but my roommate Terry Dunlavy and my cousin Sally Brownson were active in many organizations and student events.

Terry Dunlavy

Sally Brownson

Thomas Holewinski

Patsy Dunlavy

Thomas "Tom" Holewinski, a close friend of Terry's, also became a part of our inner circle. Tom had attended Sacred Heart Seminary, Oneida, WI, also, and Tom and Terry had become best friends.

Terry's sister Patsy chose to be a member of the Gamma Sigma Sorority.

Iota Fraternity sponsored the Song Festival annually. It also helped Delta Phi Sorority present the Sadie Hawkins Dance.

Sally became a member of the Kappa Gamma Sorority. Her sorority took first place in Lyceum Fraternity's Vod-Vil for their performance of "Paunchy Pete and His Performing Puppets."

The A Division debate team took first place honors at all their meets.

Russell, Patsy, Terry, Tom, and I all belonged to the

Newman Club, a campus Catholic religious group.

We attended Mass at a Catholic Church located a few blocks south of Mrs. Brahe's boarding home. Father John Patrick Feeney, brother of Joe Feeney the tenor singer of "The Lawrence Welk Show," was pastor at this church. I avoided having Father Feeney hear my confession. College students told stories of Father Feeney getting all heated up during their confessions with him. At times he went right into their part of the confessional and did all sorts of things, like yelling at them and grabbing them.

Iota's "Chick Chance" booth, offering a chance to win chickens, won first place at Lambda Chi's Campus Carnival.

Marilyn Schroeder and John Van Dyke made appearances in both student dramas, Arthur Miller's *The Crucible* and the Arabian Nights' *Aladdin*. Professor Maysell Evans directed *The Crucible*, a play revealing injustice to the witches in the Salem witch craft trials. Modern dancers enhanced *Aladdin* with their portrayals of the Slaves of the Ring and the Slaves of the Lamp.

Terry and Sally belonged to the OSC Language Club. In order to be able to join the club a student needed to be taking a foreign language class or be a foreign student. Sally was studying French and Terry Latin. Sally was an officer of the club. Somehow, I became part of the club even though I wasn't a foreign language student. I think Terry got me in.

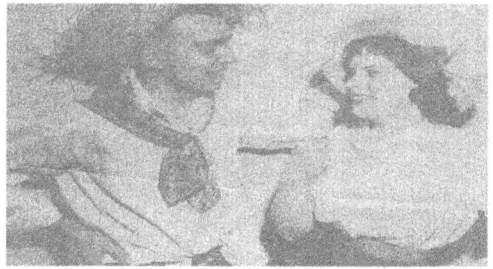

Terry in the "Spanish Fiesta"

Terry played a role in the "Spanish Fiesta" all school dance. The decorations for the dance featured colorful murals on a Mexican theme. Over 200 students attended the dance.

A Latin banquet was held at Radford Hall, with a Latin

Terry and Mary Beth Siewert in the Latin play

play called *Perseus and Andromeda*. I portrayed a priest in the banquet. Slaves served guests reclining in Roman style. The chicken was delicious.

Terry encouraged Tom and I to help out with make-up on *The Oshkosh Advance,* OSC's college newspaper. Terry was associate editor and Tom feature writer. Patsy was also a staff member.

Pollock House took first place in house decorations for the Titans 1957 Homecoming, and the Vet's float, "Eat 'Em Alive," won first place. Queen Marcia Strouf reigned over the

Homecoming activities made perfect with a 6-0 victory over the Eau Claire Blugolds.

Iota won the Kappa Gamma play contest with their play entry entitled "If Men Played Cards as Women Do." Sally

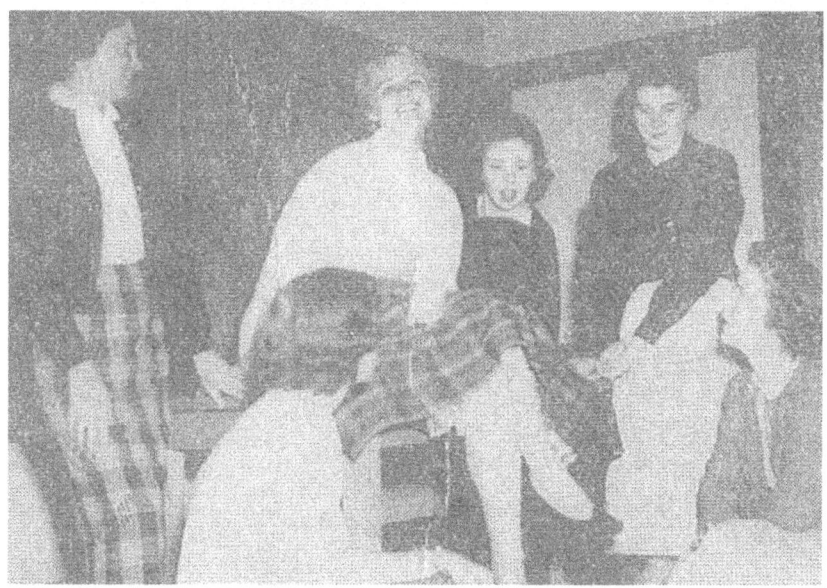

A scene from the Kappa Gamma play, starring, left to right, Phyl Gould, Sally Brownson, Shelby Lemke, Bev Broehm, Pauline Connelley, Ginny Bartz.

starred in Kappa Gamma's play, "Lavender Changes to a Red Pepper." The proceeds were given as a scholarship to a junior student.

The oriental theme, "Jasmine and Jade," was the title chosen for the 1958 OSC Prom. Dave Harmsen and Lorna Roeder reigned as Prom King and Queen over the dance festivities.

The OSC Titans football team had their best season in years, with four wins and three losses. They finished fourth in the Wisconsin State College Conference. Terry Tighe proved to be one of Coach Bob Kolf's best players.

Under Coach Eric Kitzman the Titans basketball team finished fifth in the Wisconsin State College Conference. The team had excellent balance this year. Tom O'Brien and Don Halverson led the team, with Halverson being an excellent shot. Halverson and O'Brien were classed as the greatest scorers to date in the history of the school.

MEMORIES

I remember working for Uncle Clarence on the Outagamie County highways.
I remember Uncle Clarence checking up on the work progress of the summer help.
I remember Uncle Clarence driving up just when we did something wrong.
I remember going with Gerald and Arlene to adult baseball games.

The Summer of '58

Once my freshman year of college was finished and I had moved back home to Shiocton, I needed another summer job to earn money for college.

The Outagamie County Highway Department hired college students for summer jobs. Russell had already been working for the County a couple summers.

Uncle Clarence was the Highway Commissioner for the Outagamie County Highway Department. Uncle Elmer was a foreman on one of the road crews. Pa talked to Uncle Clarence and got me a job.

Jerry Ratsch and Bill La Croix also got jobs with the County.

Pa gave me a ride to work to the County garage. It was located on the south end of River Street on the west side of the street next to a tavern. Pa worked at the Post Office on the same side of the street a few blocks north of the County garage.

The summer college guys gave Uncle Clarence a rough time. Bill La Croix let a roller he operated get out of control. He jumped off as it catapulted down a steep hill and overturned. Uncle Clarence came on the scene just as it happened and lectured and yelled at Bill after the fact. Uncle

Clarence gave me a long talk about checking the oil on the roller I operated after he found out I threw a rod in Pa's car.

I operated a roller on Uncle Elmer's road crew. The roller had huge tires for compacting gravel. As the men operating the graders moved the gravel back and forth from one side of the road to the other, I needed to follow with the roller to compact it.

The first thing to do each morning on the job was to check the gas and oil and fill if deemed necessary.

As I drove the roller up and down the graveled road, I often got too close to the edge of the road and got stuck. When I got stuck, a grader had to pull me out. Uncle Clarence showed up and asked me what I was up to. Nonetheless, he let me keep rolling all summer long.

After the graveled road was all compacted, it was sprayed with hot oil and then hot mix was laid with the green machine. A large roller with two water-filled metal drums went over the hot mix to flatten it. The water prevented the drums from sticking to the hot mix.

Occasionally after work we all had a nice, cool bottle of brew.

Taking Time for Fun

There was an old saying spread around, and we took it serious-- "It is not healthy to do all work and no play." We did indeed take time for fun.

Shiocton and all the neighboring towns sponsored adult baseball games in the summer. Joe Buss had a big passion for baseball. I went to all the baseball games. I rode with Gerald and Arlene to many of the out-of-town baseball games.

After work on hot days, it felt good to take a dip in the swimming hole under the bridge or at Dyne's. Supper was first though because Ma had it waiting as you walked in the door.

Going to the homecomings at Shiocton, Black Creek,

and Hortonville as well as the Outagamie County Fair at Seymour continued to be a major attraction not to be missed.

I had many friends, and we did many exciting things, like going to the movies, the rodeos in Manawa, the stock car races at Menzel's, and riding hot rods. We danced at weddings and rock band dances at the American Legion Hall and other places.

A couple of my closest friends were Porky Beyer and Gary Korth. Gary was Roger's wife Gerry's younger brother. We met at Roger's and Gerry's wedding and became good friends after the fact. Porky and I became close friends in high school and stuck together after graduating.

Roger and Gerry and family now lived next door at the old Ed Johnson farm, and Carl and Barbara and family lived in a mobile home on the south lot of our yard.

I got together with Gary whenever he came along with Pete and Mert Kielbasa over to Roger's and Gerry's place.

My nephews and nieces played in the back yard often. Pa bought a set of playground equipment from the school and erected it on the edge of the back lawn. Stevie, Bruce, Kevin, Dean, David, Debbie, Darrell, and Duane made good use of the playground equipment.

Stevie came over the most. Besides swinging and tee-tottering, Stevie played in our small swimming pool and

Mary, Stevie, and I in the swimming pool

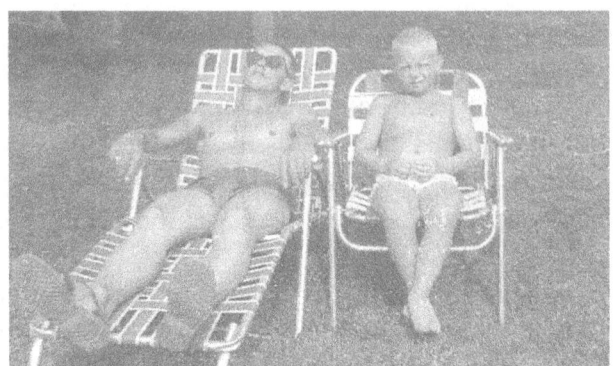
Stevie and I reclining in the sun

reclined in the sun with Mary and I. He rode the school bus with Mary. Stevie's favorite activity, however, was coming over to Grandma Cele's kitchen for a delicious donut or slice of homemade bread.

MEMORIES

I remember always having problems with residency approval of Mrs. Brahe's boarding house.
I remember the exciting field trips in Dr. Shapiro's conservation class.
I remember the thrilling dissections in Dr. Reed's zoology lab.
I remember Professor Evan's speech class.
I remember Professor Madison's English class going on a field trip to a Chicago theatre.
I remember getting my first A in a college course.
I remember going to plays in Milwaukee and Chicago.
I remember joining Iota.
I remember home knit sweaters made by Mrs. Brahe.
I remember living in the basement at Mrs. Brahe's.

A Rebounding Sophomore

I don't know when I bought a car but it must have been during my sophomore year of college. Whenever I was unable to get a ride to Oshkosh is when I got a car.

As soon as I arrived in Oshkosh for my second year of college (1958-1959), I checked in at Mrs. Brahe's, moved my paraphernalia to the upper floor, registered, and picked up my books at the rental library.

Terry and Patsy Dunlavy arrived a few days earlier. Mrs. Brahe had acquired another student to take Russell's Place, his name I don't recall. He bunked on the end where Russell had been.

Terry registered before I did, and it was a stroke of luck again for me. When he went to the station for residence approval, Mrs. Brahe wasn't on the list again for approved residences. Terry called Mrs. Brahe, and she made a few calls again to get it taken care of. I don't know why there was always such a problem with the residency approval because Mrs. Brahe operated and managed a respectable household for boarders and college students.

Even though I had a car, I walked to school because

parking on or near campus tended to be congested and difficult. I drove my car if the weather became blustery.

My course load for my sophomore year at OSC included: English 106a and 106b (English Literature), three credits per semester; History 101a and 101b (United States History), three credits per semester; English 109 (Advanced Composition), three credits; Psychology 101 (General Psychology), three credits; Speech 105 (Fundamentals of Speech), three credits; Biology 212 (Conservation), three credits; and, Biology 12a and 12b (General Zoology), five credits per semester. My total credits per semester totaled 17 credits.

John Mook

Dr. John Mook taught the General Psych class. It was a fun class, but the tests were difficult. The tests consisted of multiple choice or true and false questions. The questions were tricky, at least for me.

Paul Frazier

Professor Paul Frazier schooled me in advanced composition. It proved to be an OK class.

Jacob Shapiro

My Conservation teacher was Dr. Jacob Shapiro. I didn't master all the concepts of conservation in the classroom, but the field trips to lakes, ponds, and shorelines turned out to be a great adventure. I loved walking along the shoreline doing the conservation studies.

Edward Noyes

Gerald Reed

I studied U.S. History under Dr. Edward Noyes. I learned many things about animals in Dr. Gerald Reed's zoology classes. The dissection of animal specimens in lab was the best part of the class. What a thrill it was for the zoology student to examine the vital organs of a live, sedated frog or a preserved fetal pig. Or, was it?

Maysel Evans

Professor Maysel Evans taught us all about the fundamentals of speaking. We worked with all types of speaking. Our class room featured a small stage, and each class member had to give a speech on stage at least once a week. Each week Professor Evans lectured on the speech of the week, did the speech, and then we all took turns doing the speech of the week. We rated each other in our speech performance. It was a fun class, and we all learned how to speak in the proper way. I always had butterflies in my stomach as I went up stage but once I started it went smoothly. Speech class turned out to be one of my best courses. Miss Evans became one of my best and favorite teachers, and she was well-liked by all the students on campus. She directed some of the student dramas.

Thomas Madison

The best class of all during my sophomore year of college though had to have been my English literature course taught by Professor Thomas Madison. Terry and I were in the same class hour of this course.

The highlight of the course centered on our study of George Bernard Shaw's play *Pygmalion*. We read *Pygmalion* aloud in class, word for word. Our professor told us about the Broadway musical *My Fair Lady*, based on the play *Pygmalion*. The musical was on a six-year Broadway run.

The story of the play and musical concerns a snobbish English professor (Henry Higgins) taking on a common flower girl (Eliza Doolittle) and transforming her into a fine lady. It's all British accents and British dialects.

The most exciting part of all of this is the entire English lit class went to a Chicago theatre to see *My Fair Lady* in a live stage performance. What a thrill! What a class! What a play! Just imagine-- a young farm boy from Shiocton at a major Broadway play in a Chicago theatre. Our class had the wonderful experience of seeing and hearing professional actors singing songs from the musical on the live stage, songs like "The Rain in Spain," "On the Street Where You Live," and "Get Me to the Church on Time." We saw gorgeous costumes and beautiful sets. We heard large production numbers and glorious music. We sat way up in the balcony, if you call it sitting. Half of the time we were standing.

Dr. Reed drove Terry, three female students, and I to the Chicago theatre and back.

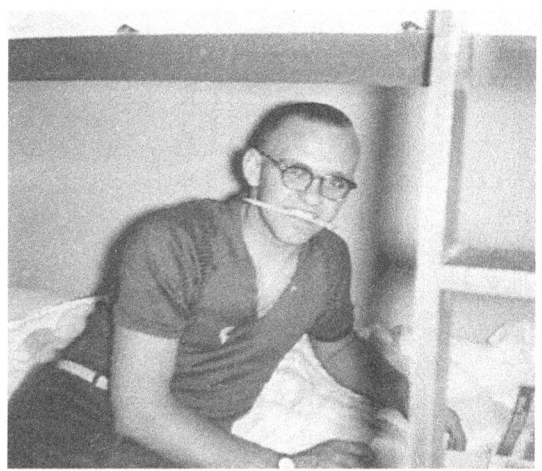
Studying hard

It was strange I failed Dr. Edward Noyes' U.S. History class one semester and excelled in it another semester. I earned a B grade in it the second semester. I also earned B grades in Dr. Reed's zoology classes and Professor Evans' speech class. I received passing grades in my conservation, Advanced Comp, and General Psych classes. I excelled in Professor Madison's English classes, getting an A grade both semesters. I had earned my first A in college. Once more I had attained a grade point average high enough to return to OSC the next year.

Campus Spotlight

Many more friends and relatives from Shiocton

attended OSC during my sophomore year, namely Sue Andrews, Pat Kennedy, C.J. Van Patten, and cousin Sandra Brownson. Cousin Sally was a junior and Bill Herminath a sophomore. I encountered many of them in the corridors of Dempsey Hall. Bill had a room at a residence on Jackson Street a few blocks north of Mrs. Brahe's residence. I stopped over at Bill's a few times, and we went to the movies on a few occasions.

After going to see the Chicago live-stage performance of the musical *My Fair Lady,* I was enthralled with theatrical live stage shows. Just imagine-- a farm boy from Shiocton excited about the theatre. Terry, Tom, and I went to see plays in Milwaukee and Chicago. Tom provided the means of travel. Tom commuted from his parents' home in Neenah, WI, with a Volkswagen. Riding in a VW is more comfortable than it looks, even all the way to Milwaukee and Chicago.

One of the most memorable plays we went to starred Alfred Lunt and Lynn Fontanne. What a thrill!

The theatre-in-the-round was exciting, too. It featured a central stage surrounded by the audience and required no stage curtain and not much scenery or props. The actors popped in and out through aisles in the audience seating. *Our Town* was one of the plays we went to in the theatre-in-the-round.

Forrest R. Polk, after 43 years of service to OSC since 1931, retired from the Presidency of Oshkosh State College.

Our head librarian and associate professor of library science at OSC, Miss Helen Wahoski, became the 1958 Wisconsin Librarian of the Year, receiving the award from the Wisconsin Library Association at its annual banquet.

Helen Wahoski

A new women's dormitory, Webster Hall, was completed in 1958 and the Reeve Memorial Union in 1959.

Terry's sister Patsy of Clintonville, WI, graduated with a B.S. degree in secondary education, with majors in English and Library Science and a minor in mathematics. She led a very active college life. Patsy was a member of the Gamma Sigma sorority for three years, Newman Club three years, the *Quiver* staff three years, the *Advance* staff four years, and honor resident two years.

Terry and I pledged Iota Alpha Sigma fraternity, and

Iota Alpha Sigma

we were received into the fraternity during formal rushing week. Iota submitted an entry into the Homecoming parade, sponsored a candidate for Homecoming Queen, participated in Lyceum's Vod-Vil, and joined their sister sorority Delta Phi in presenting the annual Sadie Hawkins dance. Dr. Reed was our fraternity's advisor.

Terry and I in a scene from "The Ransom of Red Chief"

Terry and I starred in Iota's "The Ransom of Red Chief" entry in the Kappa Gamma play contest, and we chaired Iota's "Chip Gyp" entry in the Campus Carnival. Terry was chairman of Iota's Songfest.
Sally's Kappa Gamma sorority, sponsor of the Play Contest, took first place with their "The Wizard of OSC" entry in Lyceum's Vod-Vil.
Miss Maysel Evans directed Clarence Day's comedy "Life With Mother." This presentation by the Oshkosh College Players centered around Mother Day's comical attempts to

**Dave Marshall and Marilyn Schroeder
in "Life With Mother"**

to provide an engagement ring for her son to give to his girlfriend. Marilyn Schroeder and Dave Marshall played the lead roles of Mother and Father Day.

    The annual Children's Play production turned out to be *Sleeping Beauty*. Sally portrayed the fairy Preona.

Scene from *Sleeping Beauty*. Sally Brownson, second from left, plays the fairy Preona.

Terry, Tom, and Patsy continued to work on make-up for the *Advance*, OSC's bi-monthly newspaper. Terry also worked on page layouts for the *Quiver*, OSC's yearbook. He was assistant editor of the *Quiver* this year.

Terry also enlisted Jerome "Jerry" Heiss as a helper with make-up on the *Advance*. Jerry was another friend of Terry's from Sacred Heart Seminary in Oneida, WI. Jerry also rented a room at Mrs. Brahe's.

Tom, Terry, Jerry, and I joined Newman Club and Sue Andrews joined Wesley.

Queen Marilyn Schroeder reigned over OSC's Homecoming festivities-- the colorful parade, the bonfire, the game, the open house at Pollock House, and the annual Alumni Homecoming dance. Lyceum took first place in the parade with their slogan, "Our Team's a Real Gasser," and Webster Hall won first place in house decorations with their entry, "It'll Be a Hare Raising Event." The Titan 19-8 win over Platteville fulfilled the students' high hopes for a victory.

"Snowflake Fantasy," a sorority-fraternity Christmas formal was sponsored by Gamma Sigma, Kappa Gamma, my fraternity Iota, and other societies. I took a date to the formal.

"Fontessa," OSC's 1959 Prom, provided students with the opportunity to dance modern, abstract art forms in the gym decorated in shades of blue.

The Titan gridders had their most successful season in the last 23 years. Coach Bob Kolf's Titan footballers clad in yellow and black made a season debut by defeating Northland College 44-0. Their winning streak continued as they beat UW-M's Cardinals 22-0. Next the Titans suffered losses to Stevens Point's Pointers and to Whitewater. Terry Tighe led the team in defeating Superior next. The Homecoming win over Platteville boosted the students' high spirits. The Titans did a showing at the season finale, putting down Stout 35-14. They tied with Whitewater for third place in the Wisconsin State College Conference.

Coach Kitzman's OSC cagers, on the other hand, had a disastrous basketball season ending up in an eighth place tie with Stout for the Wisconsin State College Conference.

House Life

I purchased a record player and put it on a stand by the wall alongside my bed. It included a cover to serve as a carrying case and had the capacity to play LP's and 45 rpm's.

I only used my record player when Terry wasn't in the room. We didn't need two record players going at the same time.

We played records over and over again, often listening

to Tommy Edwards' "It's All in the Game," Johnny Mathis' "Misty" or "Chances Are," and Della Reese's "Don't You Know."

I stopped at Evan's music shop most days on my walk home from campus, just to check on any new sales deals. I was able to buy many 45 rpm's at Evan's at a modest price.

I enrolled in the Columbia Music Club. The Club gave three or four LP's free for joining. I had to buy three or four albums per year to keep active in the Club, but there were many appealing ones to choose from.

Mrs. Brahe took a notion to knit sweaters for Terry and I. We had to pick out the pattern and buy the yarn. Mrs. Brahe ended up knitting three or four sweaters for each of us. The sweaters were heavy and thick. One of my sweaters had wide bands, layers, or stripes of dark brown, light brown, and white. Another one of my sweaters was one solid, tan color.

Where's the Popcorn? Terry and I went to the movies on campus on Sunday nights. We viewed old and classic films. We thought about taking along some popcorn to chew on at the showings. When we asked Mrs. Brahe, she gave us the ok. Mrs. Brahe and the ladies smelled the aroma of the popcorn as we made it, and they thought we were going to give them some. We were naïve, however, exiting out the back door with the popcorn we made. Mrs. Brahe told us how disappointed she and the ladies had been when they didn't get to taste the popcorn. From then on, we always made an extra dish for the ladies.

Terry and I went to the movies at the downtown theatres, too. We sat in the balcony and watched Rosalind Russell perform in *Auntie Mame,* a story of a young, orphaned boy named Patrick left in the care of his eccentric Aunt Mame. Actually, we laughed so much and so hard it hurt. Another movie we enjoyed immensely was *All Mine to Give,* starring Glynis Johns, Cameron Mitchell, a pioneer story of six children abandoned after their parents die, leaving the eldest to find homes for them on Christmas Day. It actually moved you to tears as you watched it.

One other movie I liked was *Yours, Mine, and Ours,* starring Lucille Ball, Henry Fonda, and Van Johnson, a comical story about a couple (Frank and Helen) marrying with eighteen children, Frank bringing 10 and Helen 8 to the marriage, and the tensions developing afterwards. My favorite, however, was *The Helen Morgan Story*, starring Ann Blyth, Paul Newman, a story of the life of the torch singer Helen Morgan. Just imagine-- a young farm boy from Shiocton enjoying the moody songs of a lady in a red dress atop of an organ.

One Sunday I spent the entire day at the movie theatres.

I did hospice care at Mrs. Brahe's. One of the ladies had to rock back and forth a few times to get up out of her chair. Eventually she became unable to care for herself but didn't want to go to a nursing home. Mrs. Brahe asked Terry and I if we were willing to help out. We said yes. We were paid a stipend for doing it. We helped her in and out of her chair and bed, plus we helped her with going to the bathroom. We lifted her onto the toilet and off when done, after Terry wiped her buttocks. Our hospice duties were short-lived. It wasn't long before she had to be given professional help.

Where's the Needle? One day I turned on my record player and discovered, to my dismay, it didn't work. As I examined it, I found out the needle part was missing. I searched all over for it with no luck. Someone took it out. My music must have been too loud or else I played too much rock music. It wasn't Terry but rather my other roommate. I was upset enough to quit school. I hid my anger inside myself though and didn't let it show. I talked to Terry about it and to Ma about it, but I had to decide on my own course of action. I told Mrs. Brahe about it, and she understood my concern but didn't take sides.

Mrs. Brahe, however, offered the use of a room downstairs in the basement. I accepted her offer. I had a nice cozy room all to myself. I was able to use the room as much as I wanted, but I still had to sleep upstairs at night. I moved my personal items downstairs to this room.

Mrs. Brahe said she heard the music from below, and it sounded nice. I made sure to keep the volume low from then on.

Soon after I moved downstairs, the needle part appeared on my bed. Relations between me and my roommate were not strained. We never talked about it. We were both naïve about it, both for not talking it out with each other, me for playing the music so loud, him for taking out the needle part instead of talking it out, me for moving down to the basement. Nonetheless, we were civil and friendly.

Occasionally Mrs. Brahe's two sons Tom and Neil stopped over for a visit. Sometimes they had something to eat. They usually came on Saturday. I think Neil was a dentist and Tom a lawyer or businessman. They were big, husky, great-hearted men.

MEMORIES

I remember going to Mary's dance recital.
I remember Len Clausen's limerick.
I remember Gary Korth.
I remember Roger and Verona Rueden's barn ablaze.
I remember Eben Rexford's rock.
*I remember working on an Outagamie County Highway
    Dept. oil truck with Jack Murphy.*
I remember visiting Terry in Door County.
*I remember the passing on of Bill Oaks, Grandma Minnie,
    and Grandpa Len.*

The Summers of '59, '60, and '61

Dance Recital

My sister Mary, cousin Bernadette Brownson, and Michael Ratsch enrolled in dance class. They learned how to dance ballet and tap.

Attending the dance recital was a thrill. All the dancing students wore colorful dancing outfits, at least one for ballet and one for tap.

I enjoyed watching the dancers do all their routines, especially Mary and Bernadette. I loved watching Michael Ratsch tap dance to the tune of "Me and My Shadow."

Buddies

I had a large circle of friends and buddies. Some of them were my first cousins. We enjoyed good times together.

My friends included: Eddie Klitzke, Gary "Beaver" Lemere, Gene Conradt, Bob Knoke, Bob Kelley, Don Huse, John "Porky" Beyer, John Johnson, Bob Brownson, Mark

Brownson, Jack Huse, John Van Straten, Joe Van Straten, Tom Van Straten, Dick Van Straten, Jack Andrews, Gary Korth, and Len Clausen.

Some of us, John Johnson and Porky Beyer included, made treks to Appleton to get pizza.

Len Clausen always enjoyed reciting a little limerick. It went like this: "Daniel Boone shot a coon, when he was only three."

On one occasion, a bunch of us, Beaver Lemere and Eddie Klitzke included, went cruising on a Friday night, ending up at a lodge or cottage in northern Wisconsin. I think we ended up at Crandon.

When I went to town during this period of my life at the age of 20, I most often drove a vehicle, either a tractor, truck, or car.

I always stopped by the stone at the Congregational

Church, Eben Rexford's rock. A bronze memorial plaque built into the rock included a quotation, "To everyone God gives a share of work to do, sometime, somewhere."

I passed the time during the summer earning money for college, hanging out with my friends and buddies, attending baseball games, going to homecomings and fairs, swimming, riding with Pa in the countryside, and having fun on family picnics.

We went to Van Straten family reunions every few years. Some were held on Grandpa Len's and Grandma

Minnie's front lawn. A big tent was put up for protection from the sun and the rain. Other reunions were held at the St. Denis church hall, the American Legion clubhouse, or Hamlin Park.

Sister Lurana played softball with us at family gatherings. She wore a heavy, black garment, and it reached all the way down to her shoes. The headgear included a hard, vinyl head piece covered with a black veil. I was intrigued with the oversized wooden rosary attached to her garment. Sister Lurana always sweat so much when she played ball with us. She was delighted when the new nun's outfits came out.

They were not as heavy, knee-length, and the vinyl head piece had disappeared.

An Unfortunate Incident

My friend Gary Korth had an accident. As a result he became paralyzed, crippled, and confined to a wheelchair. He was no longer able to care for himself.

Gary lived at his sister Mert Kielbasa's residence for a short time after the accident. Mert and Gary's wife Jerry helped the care for Gary as much as possible, but soon Gary had to be moved to a nursing facility to receive better care. I visited Gary a few times until he was moved to Tucson, Arizona. I didn't see Gary after he moved there.

Roger, Gerry, and Pa made stops to see Gary on

occasion.

When Pa and his first cousin Harold Van Straten arrived in Tucson, March, 1973, on a trek out West, Gary and Jerry picked them up at the bus depot. Gary and Jerry lived on an old Spanish Trail Road and drove 10 miles to get them. Pa and Harold stayed overnight with them, enjoyed a couple delicious meals, and appreciated their hospitality.

When Harold, Henry, and Glen Van Straten, Ray Gleason, and Pa stopped in Tucson, February, 1974, on another of Pa's treks out West, Gary and Jerry and their six month old baby Randy visited with them for two hours at the bus depot. Pa said Gary enjoyed visiting with them and asked many questions.

Passing Glimpses

In 1959 Pa lost a true friend and colleague, William "Bill" Oaks. They had worked side by side in the mail room for 34 years. Bill was still working at the Post Office when he died.

Pa's mother died on December 5, 1958 and his dad died on January 24, 1959. They both died at home. Russell sat with Pa at their bedside during their last hours.

Pa's loss, especially his parents, had great effect on him. He was sad for a long time. Ma encouraged him and helped him to move on with his life.

I didn't notice what Pa was feeling because I was involved in school. I only went to the funerals. I viewed Grandpa and Grandma at the funeral home with difficulty, just as I had Uncle Clark. We prayed the rosary at the wakes. We don't seem to follow this tradition of praying the rosary at funerals anymore. I prayed for Grandpa, Grandma, and Uncle Clark for many years after they died.

Pa retired from the Postal Service in 1961. He was honored with a dinner and awards at the American Legion Clubhouse.

The Painted Pony

Everyone liked our painted pony, and we had some exciting times with it. Mary rode the painted pony.

Mary astride the painted pony (1961)

Rueden's Barn Ablaze

When Roger and Gerry lived next door on the Ed Johnson farm, a fire started in Roger Rueden's barn. I didn't have anything to do with it. I wasn't even around when it happened. I stopped playing with matches by gas tanks after starting the fire at Uncle Clark's.

Roger Rueden's wife Verona, upon noticing the fire, flagged down a farmer riding by on a tractor.

When Roger and his brother-in-law Pete Kielbasa saw the smoke, they rushed over to get the livestock out of the blazing barn. They saved two pigs and 50 chickens.

Hundreds of bales of straw became consumed by the raging fire.

On the Road Again

I worked all three summers for Uncle Clarence and the Outagamie County Highway Department. They assigned me to a different job. No more driving the roller and getting stuck, and no more work with Uncle Elmer. I now worked with the Everett Spoehr gang. They made new roads or improved old roads, but they didn't use a green machine. They made or improved roads with the use of graders, an oil truck, and a steel drum roller.

Ben Bates and Loy Bricco operated the graders. Loy was Everett Spoehr's son-in-law. Ben and Loy were excellent graders, the best ever. Jack Murphy operated the oil truck, and I was his assistant.

The first work detail in building a new road was to create a hard base with the use of the graders and the roller.

The next step encompassed hauling loads and loads of gravel and dumping them on the hard base. When this was being done, I was the flagman and had the job of stopping oncoming traffic from both directions and routing them through. It was an easy job, a fun job, and it gave me a sense of authority.

Next, Ben and Loy started grading the gravel, moving it from side to side.

Next, Jack Murphy and I started adding oil to the gravel. Jack drove, and I manipulated the lever at the back of the truck. Jack motioned with his arm when to start and when to quit spraying. Once, the lever stuck and Jack had to stop the truck and quickly come back to stop the spray. From then on when the lever stuck, I knew how to fix it. When the lever stuck, you just had to hit it hard to move it.

A semi truck full of hot oil satisfied our oil supply needs. We used a long, wide (approximately 4 inches) hose to suck the hot oil from the semi into our oil truck. Once the hot oil was added to our oil truck, gas-fired heat under the oil drum kept it hot, but we sprayed it out almost immediately anyway. We used insulated rubber gloves because the heat was intense while handling the hose. Even with insulated gloves the hose was almost too hot to handle.

I needed to keep track of how much oil we added to the gravel in a small ledger. At any moment my boss, Mr. Spoehr, asked how much oil had been added. Jack told me Mr. Spoehr was impressed with how I kept such good figures.

We kept adding hot oil to the gravel, now also known as hot mix, until it had enough consistency. We often had to reload more hot oil from the semi in order to have enough to add to the hot mix. We had to coordinate this with the boss because we didn't want any hot oil left in the oil drum. Oil left over in the oil drum became difficult to reheat.

The graders continued to mix the hot mix as we sprayed more oil onto it until it was completely ready to level out as a new road.

I became very dirty on my arms and face from the oil spraying. I had to use a special cream to clean my skin.

After the oil spraying was completed, Jack and I, and even the boss on occasion, leveled some parts of the hot mix on the edges before rolling started.

We took pride in the finished product. Mr. Spoehr's roads were the best of any, and Uncle Clarence knew and appreciated it.

On rainy days we rode in the orange company van. We used the brooms and shovels, housed in the van, to clean and sweep intersections.

Mr. Spoehr picked me up and dropped me off at home with the orange van. I didn't have to drive to work.

Jack and I became close friends. I slept over at Jack's

place in Hortonville a few times.

A Trek to Door County

At the end of summer, I went to Door County to visit my college roommate Terry Dunlavy and stay for the weekend. Ma didn't want me to go, but I talked her into letting me go.

When I arrived in Fish Creek, I had some car trouble. Oh, no, I thought, Ma had told me not to go. Terry and I

Terry Dunlavy

discovered the brake lever had been pushed in and locked. What a stroke of luck! It wasn't anything serious.

Terry had a summer job at the Fish Creek Motel and Cottages. He helped serve meals, and boarded in one of the cottage rooms. He made room for me to sleep in his room during my brief visit.

We took in a play at the Peninsula Players Theatre in a Garden. It was a wonderful experience. Live drama on stage had become a favorite thing for us. After the play, we went to a nightclub nearby to see and hear the actors sing and perform. What a thrill!

At the end of the weekend, Terry packed up his belongings, and I drove him home to Clintonville to spend a few days with his family before returning to Oshkosh to start another semester at OSC.

MEMORIES

I remember the family trips of 1959.
I remember a 1966 school bus trip to Glenwood City and to Shawano Lake.

A Traveling They Did Go

Pa and the family traveled often before and after he retired. Pa's brothers, cousins, and friends also went on many of his trips with him. Since I was occupied with my college studies, I wasn't able to travel with Pa on most of these trips.

A Third Trip South, 1959

Ma and Pa went on a third trip south in 1959 from March 3 to March 16, taking along Joyce, Alice, Karen, Mary, and Lennie. All seven rode in a 1959 black four-door Chevrolet. The roads were rough, and it snowed all the way, seven times on the first day. They put up in a room with four beds in a motel at Rockville, Indiana, 420 miles from home, at a cost of $11.

Snow continued until they arrived at Vincennes, Indiana. They boarded, after another 415 miles, in a motel at Mt. Eagle, Indiana, for $8.

Another 432 miles put them at Perry, Georgia. It rained all day, the motel at this location cost $8, too.

They traveled through hundreds of miles of Georgia pines and stopped at the Swanee River and the Stephen Foster home.

Once in Florida, they drove through orange and grapefruit groves. Workers along the way picked fruit by the vanloads from September to June.

Pa rented a home at Lake Wales for five days at a cost of $60. They visited Tampa, Clearwater Beach, St. Petersburg, the big Sunshine Bridge, and the Atlantic Ocean. They went swimming a few times.

Pa bought 12 bags of fruit for $16.50 to take home.

Chrysanthemums ans peach trees were all abloom. The temperatures ranged from 61 to 80 degrees.

Once they reached Wisconsin on the trip home, the roads were snowbound. The motels were open, but they were unable to get off the road because of the five-foot deep drifts. Pa drove to keep everyone warm. Cars were stuck in the snow. Somehow Pa got everyone home safe, but the driveway was full of snow four feet high. Needless to say, it took some time yet to get the car up to the house.

A Trip North, 1959

Ma and Pa, accompanied by Joyce, Alice, Karen, and Mary, traveled north from July 15 to July 17. Pa drove the 1959 black four-door Chevrolet on this trip, too. They ate some meals on roadside tables made of cedar.

At St. Ignace, Michigan, they rode a boat over the straits to Mackinac Island. They stayed overnight at St. Ignace in two motel rooms at a cost of $7 per room.

At Sault St. Marie, they viewed huge boats go through the locks.

The next stop was Iron Mountain. Two motel rooms there cost $6 each. On a beach near Manistique, they took a dip in Lake Michigan.

Moving on to Florence, Wisconsin, they viewed the world's largest ski jump, 313 feet, and the world's largest pump in an abandoned mine.

When they arrived at Mercer, Wisconsin, they drove

out to see the 310 hunting shanty. It was a terrible sight to behold. It hadn't been used for two seasons.

A stop at Shrimp's animal exhibit thrilled everyone. The animals, birds, and fish were so lifelike.

One last stop occurred at the fish hatchery in Woodruff, Wisconsin.

The black Chev stalled at Marion, Wisconsin, during heavy rains, but it only turned out to be a loose coil wire.

A School Bus Trip to Glenwood City, 1966

Pa had purchased one of the school buses from the

Shiocton School District. Pa had the motor engine overhauled, and he remodeled the inside of the bus. All of the seats, except three, were removed. A few seats needed to be left for riding. Bunk beds, a closet, heater, stove, and curtains were added.

Seven of us, Al, Celia, Joyce, Alice, Karen, Lennie, and I, took a four-day school bus trip, June 7-10, to Glenwood City, Wisconsin. We made the 220-mile trek to Glenwood City in seven hours.

Aunt Florence, married to Bill Sands, saw us drive up to their greenhouse. They had a son named Terry. A grandson, Todd, was staying with them for the summer. They were busy working at their greenhouse.

We parked our school bus in their driveway for the two nights we stayed. We slept in the bus and ate in their house. We played games of rummy with Florence.

We visited Bill's parents at Menominee and went to their cottage on Lake Trainor. Pa caught seven croppies, and we took them with us.

When Pa lit it, the gas oven in the stove in our school bus gave off a big bang, but there was no fire.

On the way back home, we stopped at Aunt Edna's and Uncle Heinie's at Shawano Lake and cooked and ate the seven croppies Pa had caught.

Our trip only cost $28. Gas cost $13.50 and food $14.50.

MEMORIES

I remember Pa's, Gug's, and Dutch's fishing adventures in Canada during the sixties.
I remember Pa talking about the black flies, mosquitoes, and Army worms in Canada.
I remember Pa's tale of a big bull moose running after them, almost up to their boat.

A Fishing They Did Go

Pa and Company went fishing in Canada almost every year for a few years. Once you have been there, it is like a magnet pulling you back again and again.

Lawrence Klitzke, Gerald, and Pa spent 10 days fishing in Ontario, Canada, in 1961, leaving June 19 and returning June 29. They rode in Pa's 1961 Chevrolet, with Gerald's 14-foot Alumacraft, trailer, and 3 ½ horse Evinrude motor. They slept in Klitzke's 10 x 12 foot tent.

The mosquitoes and black flies were thick, but OFF held them back.

At first the fish didn't bite, but when they moved to a different spot they lucked out with some good walleye bites. They all got their limit and ate walleye pike everyday for every meal, over 100. They got their limit with northerns, too.

One day they saw a marvelous sight-- a big brute of a bull moose, standing nine feet tall, must have weighed a ton, eating lily pods in the lake. He was aggressive, too. When the bull moose caught sight of them, it came running after them at a fast pace, bellowing and snorting all the time. The bull came real close to them, but they motored away from him in their boat.

One day they caught 37 perch. The next day they

caught 100 northerns and threw them all back.

Their expenses amounted to $112 total, $37 each guy.

In 1962 Pa and Gug headed up to Canada again for another fishing trip, and this time Russell went along. They took Pa's 1961 Chevrolet again and Gug's trailer and tent. The tent measured 14 x 16 feet and had a wood stove sewed into the tent floor.

They drove to Longlac, Ontario, Canada, visited their Indian guide Rano Fisher, and set up their tent at their friend Skinner's place.

They got their limits on walleyes, also caught northerns, and 40 small perch. They took home 98 pounds of frozen fish.

They nearly shot a big black bear on the highway.

They ate walleye all the time. Gug cooked pike fine.

Pa, Gug, and Dutch took along Father Van Nuland, the priest at St. Denis Parish, on their next trip to Canada in June, 1964. They set up camp near Vermilion Bay.

It rained often, but they caught a large amount of walleyes, perch, and northerns. Russell landed the biggest one, a 42-inch, 16-pound northern. He took it to a freezer 30 miles away to take home whole.

Army worms crawled everywhere. They covered the roads, but they didn't bite or sting.

It rained often, and they played cards often.

MEMORIES

I remember Pa, Gug, and Company going up to Canada each fall during the sixties to hunt moose.
I remember Pa killing a big, black bear, worth a Daniel Boone award.
I remember Pa's boat capsized and Gug dived in seven feet of lake water to retrieve the guns.

Hunting the Big Ones

Pa and Gug went moose hunting every fall every year during the sixties. Many of their friends and relatives became interested in big game and went along to hunt with them on their big game treks.

Pa and Gug had a dream for years and years to go big game hunting. They wanted to hunt moose, elk, and bear. They started fulfilling their dream in 1960.

Lawrence Klitzke and William Utke went with them on their first big game hunt in 1960. They took Gug's 1959 Chevrolet, Klitzke's 1958 Chevrolet, and a trailer.

They set up their hunting camp eight miles outside of Vermilion Bay, Ontario, Canada.

Dave Lands, a Chippewa Indian, served as their hunting guide from 8 a.m. to 5 p.m. daily.

They hunted in stands and drove the woods but saw no moose. They tried to get another guide, but he was drunk. They went home without any big game.

Pa said, in rhyme,

> "I have just got back from Vermilion Bay,
> Where I never had been before;

Ain't got as much money as I had when I left,
But I know a whole lot more."

Lawrence Klitzke, Pa, and Gug headed for Ontario in 1961 to hunt moose again. They took Gug's 1959 Chevrolet, Father Van Nuland's trailer, an aluminum 17-foot canoe, a 14-foot Alumacraft boat, Klitzke's Ford station wagon, and two 10 x 12 foot tents.

They met up with their Indian guide Rano Fisher and went into the bush 30 miles from Longlac. They set up camp on a small island in order to get away from timber wolves and bear.

The temperature was 22 degrees. Pa put on insulated underwear, a coat, pants, cap, and socks and crawled into his sleeping bag. Two gas heaters burned for heat, but Pa threw on a heavy, wool blanket yet to keep warm.

On the first day of open shooting Gerald killed a big bull moose with two shots in its chest shooting with his 30.06. It was a three-year old bull moose, about 1,200 pounds. They towed him in the water to camp and hung him in a birch tree.

A dream come true on the first day of the season. Gerald was so glad. Did the other two hunters notice a tear come from Gug's eye?

The next day Klitzke shot at a two-year-old bull moose several times. The wounded bull got away in the woods. They trailed him 300 feet and shot him down for good. They cut the 1,000 pound bull in halves and dragged them 637 yards to the boat.

Pa, after several shots to the head, got his moose the next day, an 1,100 pound cow.

Their guide Rano said, "You happy? You happy? You happy?" It was enough to make grown men laugh and cry.

It took an hour to load Gerald's bull moose. He wanted to take it home whole.

The trip cost $810. The guide cost $315, licenses $303, and gas and supplies $192. They bought 500 pounds of ice to keep the moose cold on the trip back home.

Ma and Gug's 1,200 lb. bull moose (1961)

In 1962 the same three hunters, Klitzke, Pa, and Gug, headed back up to Longlac, Ontario.

They sighted no moose for many a day. The moose didn't respond to their moose calls. Rano and Lawrence lucked out one morning as they heard one walking in the water. They paddled closer, and Lawrence put down a two-year-old bull moose with three shots. It took five hours to get the moose out. They dragged it whole to the boat, a distance of 700 yards.

On their 1963 moose hunting trek to Longlac, Pa and Gerald had a new crew accompanying them, namely Clinton Tackman, Orville Froelich, and cousin Dale Van Straten. They rode in Gerald's and Clinton's cars and took Gerald's trailer.

On the first three days of the season they no success.

On the fourth day Gerald killed a one and one-half year old bull moose with three shots from his 30.06. The moose had galloped towards them.

Clinton and Orville went home on the seventh day and took Gerald's moose along.

The next day Dale got a one and one-half year old bull moose with three shots. Later the same day Dale and Gerald put down another moose at dark. When they searched for it the next day, there was no trace of it.

Lawrence Klitzke, Clinton Tackman, and cousins Roy and Dale Van Straten went to Longlac on a 1964 hunt with Pa and Gerald.

They had a fish fry the first day from 30 walleyes the crew caught.

They were unable to go on the waters opening day because of rain and heavy winds with three-foot high waves.

Pa shot the first moose on this trip. He saw a movement at 20 rods and made a perfect hit through the lungs. It was a 600 pound, one and one-half year old nubbin moose.

The next day Clinton got a young bull moose like Pa's. It took two hours and 20 minutes to move the moose. They used a winch. This gas engine winch moved at a pace of 15 feet per minute.

Roy and Rano didn't make it back to camp one night. They spent the night under a big tree because it stormed too much to cross the lake. The wind howled all night.

Dale and Roy became the next crew members to get moose. They each shot a three-year-old bull moose.

Pa and his 600 lb. nubbin moose (1964)

Ma and three moose (Dale's, Roy's, Al's) (1964)

    Lawrence Klitzke and William Block went with Pa and Gug to Longlac on their 1965 moose hunt. They rode in Block's 1965 Chevrolet station wagon and Klitzke's 1957 Ford station wagon and took Gug's trailer.

    Pa shot a three and one-half year old bull moose weighing 1,100 pounds. Gerald got a big cow moose, about 1,200 pounds.

    After getting those two moose, no more were sighted for six days.

    Pa said again some more rhyme,

"Now after all we had great pleasure,
And bad luck, why surely not;
For the oldest hunter with us,
Says, That's when someone gets shot."

Pa, Gug, and William Block did the 1966 moose hunt. They took Gerald's 1958 Cadillac and big, yellow trailer. The trailer was loaded with about two tons of equipment, a 14 x 16 foot tent, a 9 x 9 foot tent, tarps, canvasses, a heater, a gas stove, four outboard motors, two canoes, one small scow, a 16-foot boat, a moose winch, a chain saw, rope, chairs, tackle boxes, sacks of potatoes and cabbage, rifles, suit cases, sleeping bags, and mattresses.

The first day of hunting, Pa shot a big cow moose.

On the second day, as it was getting dark, Pa saw a black thing move at about 150 yards or 30 rods away in a creek. He had to get down on his knees in the water and grass, push the grass aside, grab his gun, aim, and fire. It dropped but came up fighting and struggling. Pa took good aim and fired three more shots, and it was quiet. When he went up and approached it, he discovered it wasn't a moose but a big, black bear. The first shot hit the shoulder and the last the head. The bear had clawed the bank and log where it fell. It weighed 400 pounds and measured 6'6". Pa had killed a big, black bear. It was worth a Daniel Boone award.

On the third day Pa and Gug encountered a bull and cow moose on the road at dark. Pa hit the bull with his fourth shot, but it still moved. Pa's gun jammed, and Gerald got the shell out with his jack knife. One more shot finished the bull.

Gug and Bill got blood poisoning from black fly bites and went to a doctor for shots and pills to overcome it.

Pa had a taxidermist in Readfield, Wisconsin, make the bear hide, head, and claws into a rug. When he got the bear rug from the taxidermist, Pa hung it up on the wall above the entrance steps leading to basement in our home.

Pa and his 400 lb. black bear (1966)

    At a meeting at the Van Straten Oil Station in Shiocton, Gug, Pa, and Bill Block planned for the 1967 moose hunt.

    On this hunting trek, they took the school bus camper and Gug's yellow trailer.

    Pa and Gug went on a boat ride and encountered a big bull moose and cow, but they didn't take their guns out of their cases because the season wasn't open yet. They saw these same moose the next day as the season opened, but another hunter shot them.

A couple days later Bill had a lucky day and killed two moose. Bill and Rano had been in a canoe, Rano paddling. As they came around a bend, there stood a cow moose. Bill put her down with two shots from his 30.06. Right after shooting the cow, a five-year-old bull appeared, and Bill got him, too. After three years, or 17 days, or 90 hours, Bill had taken his moose. The bull weighed 1,200 pounds. Needless to say, Bill was proud.

The next day they celebrated with a boiled dinner and playing rummy and cribbage.

On the way back home to Shiocton the engine gave out on the school bus. The problem turned out to be two pistons with holes, a burned valve, and a cracked block. They spent the entire day at the garage, and the new block assembly cost $414.

I wonder what Uncle Clarence thought when he heard about the cracked block.

They now had two members of their hunting crew indoctrinated into famous hunting clubs. Pa now belonged to the Daniel Boone Club for killing a bear unassisted without the use of dogs, and Bill Block now belonged to the Davy Crockett Club for killing two moose within a minute.

At the end of their 1967 moose hunt, Pa, Gug, and Bill were already making plans for and eagerly looking forward to their 1968 moose hunt.

On this trek they took the school bus, yellow trailer, and Gerald's Jeep Scout pulling the gray trailer. The trailers housed all their equipment, including the two boats and two canoes.

They always stopped at Skinner's at Longlac upon arrival and got Rano. They went 20 miles into the bush to the same spot as last year.

They had boiled dinner the next night, but they didn't play cards because they were too tired.

Pa got a cramp in his right leg the next morning. It took an hour to get his foot on the floor. All the strain of doing this made Pa sweat a lot. He figured the cause of it came from too much sitting in the canoe and walking in the swamp. Yet, he went back to the canoe the next day, sitting 12 hours, and he sat nine more hours in the canoe the following day.

Some days Pa was all alone in the wilds of Canada. He had his 30.06 to protect himself from a mad charging bull moose, an ugly grizzly bear, a fierce brown bear, a savage black bear, and the vicious hungry timber wolves. If the 30.06 failed, all was lost.

They didn't get to pull their triggers on this trip, although nine moose were in their area. They saw fresh tracks every day.

Five hunters went on the 1969 moose hunt. They were Pa, Gug, Bill Block, Ron McNary, and Bill Johnson. At Pelican Lake, they picked up Merle Statezny, a friend of Bill's, and now they were six. They had two guides this time, Rano and Max Fisher.

They took the school bus and yellow trailer.

On the way out to the bush, they had a broken spring and a blowout on the big, yellow trailer.

They split up into three hunting crews, instead of two. Gug, Rano, and Pa were in the school bus. Bill Johnson, Ron, and Max set up a tent 15 miles away from the school bus. Bill Block and Merle were in another tent 10 miles away. Each crew was set up near where they hunted.

On opening day the canoe carrying Pa and Rano capsized. It was so cold, and Pa came up gasping for breath five times. His boots tangled in a lawn chair. When he came up, he was unable to see. Finally, Pa and Rano got to the boat and moved to shore with it. Gug heard their upset and came to assist. Gug saw the guns at the bottom of the river, undressed, and dived down in the seven feet of water to get them. It took an hour to get back to the tent. Pa and Rano stripped and got in their warm sleeping bags. It took all night for them to get warm. Gug worked all night on getting their wet clothes dry.

The next day Gerald had a fun day. He took down a two-year-old bull moose at 50 yards with one shot in the neck.

Soon after pulling Gug's moose across the river and dressing him out, they heard a moose call. They got in a canoe and spotted a cow and her calf at 150 yards. Gerald hit the cow, but she swam across the river to shore. The calf, meanwhile, got away into the woods. The cow stood humped up on shore, and Gerald finished her off with another shot.

It was a great day for Gerald. He had gotten a dandy bull weighing 700 pounds and a big cow weighing 900 pounds.

Merle Statezny also had a great day. He put down a 900 pound bull moose.

All their moose hunts were exciting and great experiences, even the times when they didn't see or put down a moose or when it rained for hours and hours on end. A dream realized.

After most hunts Gerald and the other hunters hung their prized game from the big trees alongside the Van Straten Oil Station property.

One year the moose hunters put on a big feed in Shiocton for the townspeople to taste the bear meat and the moose meat. This game meat had a deliciously different taste from the meat of domestic beef and pork.

MEMORIES

I remember my dream, of becoming a teacher, shattered.
I remember a semester of no progress in my college classes.
I remember the Oshkosh Titans basketball team being
*   district champs.*
I remember working at Paine Lumber Company.
I remember getting an A in a history class at OSC.

A Frazzled Junior

In the fall of 1959 I moved back in Mrs. Brahe's, registered, and started attending classes.

I made an appointment with Dr. David Bowman and

David Bowman

talked with him about getting into the School of Education to study to become a teacher. After my talk with Dr. Bowman, I decided teaching wasn't going to be my life's work.

I wasn't going to be a teacher. My dream was shattered, and my spirits were low.

I took advantage of the counseling services on campus. I guess the counseling didn't help much, but the counselor advised me to finish out the semester of registered classes and to start thinking of some other career to replace teaching. I followed the counselor's advice, but I was frustrated as I thought about what to do with the rest of my life.

My course of study for the first semester included: English 117 (American Literature), English 233 (The English Novel), History 101a (United States History), Education 326 (Philosophy of American Education), Biology 201 (Genetics), and Health Education 5 (First Aid), all three credits each, except for the one credit First Aid course. The U.S. History course was a repeat because I had failed it when I first took it in my sophomore year.

I enjoyed taking the English novel and Genetics courses. In the English novel class I was exposed to and analyzed various English novelists and novels. Genetics was very exciting because of the study of and experimentation with the fruit fly.

I passed the two English classes and the History class.

Nevertheless my studies suffered throughout because my spirits were low and I was emotionally disturbed. I kept wondering what I was going to do with my life from hereon.

Even though I liked doing the fruit fly study and learning first aid, I didn't progress well in my genetics, first aid, and education courses. I tried to withdraw from them, but it was too late. I failed all three of these courses.

I didn't register for the second semester.

Campus Spotlight, 1959-1960

The name of the college changed to Wisconsin State College at Oshkosh, with the acronym WSC-O, but it still continued to be known as Oshkosh State College or OSC.

Terry Dunlavy, my roommate, had become editor of the college's yearbook, *The Quiver*.

A new college president, Dr. Roger E. Guiles, came on

Roger Guiles

the scene at OSC. He replaced the retiring Forrest R. Polk. Dr. Guiles was faced with the problem of increased enrollments, and adding new course offerings and faculty to go along with it.

The Reeve Memorial Union was dedicated. The building became our coffeehouse and bookstore, pool room and dining hall, snack bar and music lounge, reading room and concert hall, dance hall and workshop, but most of all a place for college living, a place for OSC students to be.

Student enrollment increased to 2,084.

All the OSC students felt the spirit at the 1959 Homecoming. Defeat at the game was overcome by spirit.

Kappa Gamma had the first place float and Radford Hall first place in house decorations. Joyce Morita reigned as Queen of festivities.

The two drama productions were "The Happiest Millionaire," directed by Miss Maysel Evans, and "The Glass Menagerie," directed by Miss Gloria Link.

Kappa Gamma (for the third year in a row) won Lyceum's Vod-Vil contest with their "Marching Saints" entry.

The 1960 children's play, "The Wizard of Oz," was enjoyed by many youngsters. Annett Stern directed the play, assisted by Jane Dorn, Miss Maysel Evans, and Mr. Robert Brismaster.

The Alethean sorority's entry, "Cinderella's Slipper," won the Ice Sculpturing Contest trophy.

One of the biggest thrills of the year came when the Oshkosh Titans basketball team became the District 14 champs.

The Alethean sorority took first place for "Anastasia" in the annual Kappa Gamma Play Contest.

The 1960 prom took on the romantic and exotic theme of "Safari," with refreshments served at a jungle trading post.

Terry still remained active in the Iota fraternity.

I had dropped all college activities.

Sue Andrews became an officer in the Alethean sorority.

Lyceum acquired a house, the first fraternity house on campus.

Clemans Hall, the first men's residence hall, opened in 1960.

Another one of my brothers got married. Russell wed Geraldine "Gerri" Williamson on April 23, 1960. My brother Carl and I were groomsmen. Carl's wife Barbara was a bridesmaid.

The reception and dance were held at the American Legion Clubhouse in Shiocton.

Instead of letting everyone go to a restaurant to get something to eat, Ma, Aunt Edna, and a couple other ladies made up some sandwiches and salads to accompany the wedding cake.

People living in Shiocton were accustomed to having a snack late at night. People went to the restaurant at midnight, 1:00 a.m., or 2:00 a.m. to get something to eat. If the restaurant was closed, they had to find something to eat at home.

Ma often fixed Pa something to eat when he came home at midnight or later. She fried up some potatoes and heated up some ham or beef or fried some eggs.

Pat Dunlavy graduated from OSC in 1959 with a Bachelor of Science degree in Secondary Education. She had majors in Library Science and English and a Mathematics minor.

Terry Dunlavy graduated from OSC in 1961 with a Bachelor of Arts degree. His majors were Library Science and English and his minors Speech and Latin. He earned his Masters Degree from the University of Wisconsin, Madison, and obtained a job as manager of a branch library in New York.

By the time classes and finals ended for the first semester, I had obtained a job at Paine Lumber Company. I worked the early evening shift, from 6:30 or 7:00 p.m. until 11:00 p.m. or midnight, four or five hours.

It was satisfying work, making plywood doors. We applied glue or paste to one sheet of plywood, put another plywood sheet on top, and sent it into the heating and pressing machine. Pieces of wood measuring approximately an inch were placed between the two plywood sheets. Actually, the pieces of wood were already pre-glued to the inside of one of the plywood sheets.

Mrs. Brahe allowed me to remain a boarder, earning my room and board the same as had been done previously. Since I worked the early evening hours, I was able to be there during the day to help with meals and cleaning. I napped between meals.

I became a close friend to one of the guys working at Paine Lumber Company. I went along with him one weekend to visit his family. We got back late on Monday. I apologized to Mrs. Brahe and made up for it by doing some extra jobs for her.

I worked at Paine Lumber Company until June. During the summer months of 1960 I once more worked for Uncle Clarence and the Outagamie County Highway Dept.

I checked my status at OSC and discovered my grade point was high enough to allow me to continue attending classes at the college in the fall.

I registered and settled in for the first semester of the 1960-1961 college year. I was still classified as a junior because I only earned 12 credits during the 1959-1960 college year, having enrolled only for the first semester the same college year.

The college was growing. The college staff now included 135 instructors. Registration of students increased to 2,260. Eleven major buildings existed on campus.

I enrolled in English 216 (Continental Literature), Geology 2 (General Geology), History 204 (Europe Since 1870), Math 17 (Plane Trigonometry), and Library Science 81 (Reference and Bibliography). English, History, and Math were three credit classes. Geology was five credits and Library Science two credits.

The Geology course became too difficult for me, and I withdrew from it before it was too late. Since it was a five-credit course, I didn't want to fail it.

Eugene Moushey

Eugene Moushey taught the Reference and Bibliography course. Mr. Moushey acquainted us, his student class, with the traits of a reference librarian, the length of time to spend on a reference question, and the essential materials to include in the ready reference collection.

We came to know the needed traits of the reference librarian, including: intelligence, accuracy, professional knowledge, dependability, courtesy, resourcefulness, tact, memory, perseverance, pleasantness, cooperativeness, speed, neatness, et cetera. A reference librarian needs to be able to give the correct information when answering a question, to do accurate indexing and filing, to know where to look for information, to know the reference collection and other collections, to finish research in a timely manner, to use shortcuts and efficient methods, to pursue the question in spite of difficulties and inconveniences, to smile, to be orderly, to be neat, to be able to defend your work, and to show you know your work.

The more reference librarians become familiar with the tools of their trade and the more they use them in their daily work, the more proficient and speedier they become. Some reference questions are able to be answered quickly. More complex questions take longer to find the answer. If the question requires much research, get the contact information from the library patron to be called when the answer is found. A question may not be answerable, but before such a conclusion is made all sources need to have been examined and the question needs to have been referred to other reference staff persons, superiors, and departments.

We became very familiar with the major encyclopedias, including: *Encyclopedia Americana, Collier's, Enclopaedia Britannica, Columbia, Compton's, Lincoln Library, World Book*, and the *Canadian Encyclopedia*.

Mr. Moushey reviewed all of the handbooks and yearbooks, including: *Statesman's Yearbook, World Almanac, Whitaker's Almanac*, and the *Statistical Abstract*. All of the dictionaries, including: *Webster's, Funk and Wagnall's*, and *Roget's Thesaurus*. All the biographical dictionaries, including: *Dictionary of American Biography* and *Current Biography*. The national and trade bibliographies, including: *CBI (Cumulative Book Index), Publishers Weekly*, and *BIP (Books in Print)*. Mr. Moushey further covered directories, indexes, collections, government publications (i.e. *Monthly Catalog)*, serials (i.e. *Reader's Guide to Periodical Literature)*, pamphlets and the vertical file, maps and atlases, graphic material, and so on and so forth.

We had to memorize six check points on all of these books and materials. If we remembered the check points, we were bound to do well on the tests. The check points included: authority, scope, treatment, format, arrangement, and special features. Basically, you did well in this course if you memorized the purpose of the book or material and what it covered, how it was arranged, and how it was different from other sources.

I earned a C grade in this intensive course, a well deserved grade for all I had to learn in it.

Mr. Moushey's reference class, a very intensive one involving much memory work, was probably not the best course to introduce a person to the field of librarianship. Taking some of the general courses first, like The Library in the Community, seems a better option for the potential library science student.

I just managed to pass the trigonometry course. The

trigonometry course was much more difficult than the trigonometry I was exposed to in my high school algebra classes.

I received passing grades in the English classes I had taken.

Werner Braatz taught history extremely well. I thoroughly enjoyed his European history course. We had to buy blue exam pamphlets for taking exams in his class. Exams in Mr. Braatz' class were all essay exams. I filled one blue exam booklet and almost all of a second one. I received an A grade from Mr. Braatz. Wow! An A in a college history course.

I enrolled in five courses for the second semester, but later withdrew from all of them and from campus life.

I moved back home to Shiocton.

I took a couple six to eight week courses at the Technical College in Appleton. One was a typing class and the other a class on business machines.

I picked up a brochure at the Technical College on court reporting held at Spencerian Business College in Milwaukee.

I thought about studying to be an artist. I was skilled in sketching and drawing. I had entered a couple drawing

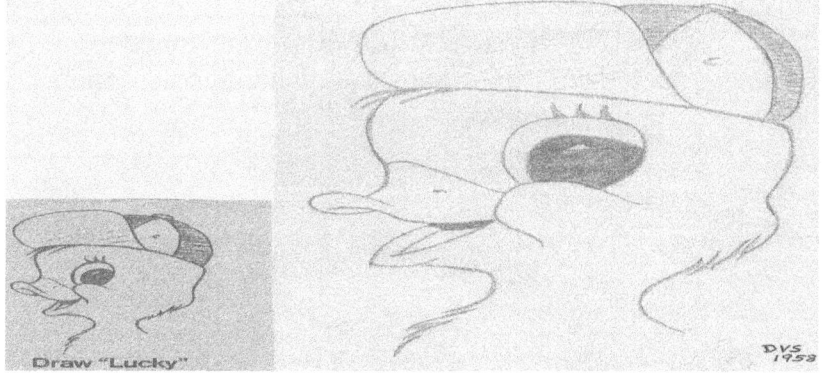

contests, and the results were excellent. Art school, however, was expensive, and I didn't know if it was a profession to rely on for steady employment.

I gave the idea of studying to be a court reporter more thought. The more I thought about it, the more I became convinced to follow up on this idea.

I worked for Uncle Clarence on the Outagamie County Highway Dept. during the summer of 1961.

I enrolled at the Spencerian Business College in Milwaukee in the fall of 1961.

I applied for and successfully secured a Knights Templar loan to help with the costs of attending Spencerian.

MEMORIES

I remember attending Milwaukee's Spencerian Business College.
I remember visiting Bill La Croix at Marquette University.
I remember learning to do shorthand on the stenotype machine.
I remember signing up for the early draft on the buddy system to serve Uncle Sam.

To Be or Not To Be

I had long been exposed to Shakespearean literature and drama. In our high school English class we read *Julius Caesar* out loud, word for word. We read and analyzed Shakespearean works in college classes, too. I read some more of William Shakespeare's plays of my own desire.

I loved *Julius Caesar*. The Ides of March ignited a spark in me to be remembered the rest of my life. Especially memorable was the scene in the play when Brutus came to pierce Julius Caesar, and Caesar said, "Et tu, Brute."

Hamlet though became my favorite play of all of Shakespeare's plays. I committed Hamlet's words to rote, especially, "To be or not to be, that is the question."

Yes, indeed, to be or not to be.

To be or not to be an artist. No, not as a profession.

To be or not to be a court reporter. This was the question I now put before me. Court reporting became my next quest.

A few weeks before the fall semester of 1961 started at Spencerian Business College in Milwaukee, I pre-registered at the business college and looked for a place to board. The college had a list of available residences for rooming.

I found a boarding place only a few blocks from the college. I boarded at a home owned by a couple of homespun ladies, with my room located adjacent to the living room and the kitchen and bathroom just down the hallway. I had been given permission to watch television in the living room at any time and had free access to the kitchen.

I purchased my own groceries, plus I brought staples along with me from Shiocton. I did my own cooking, except when the ladies invited me to eat with them. The longer I stayed there, the more often they had me eat with them. It was such a wondrous place to live, so homespun.

I had to get a permit to park my car on the street at night. I drove my car at least once a week to keep it in good running order.

I walked to school daily, except during inclement weather. Parking near the college was limited, and I ended up walking just as far as from my residence.

The ladies loved making their own sauerkraut. They had a crock for doing it. They were delighted when I brought them a big bag of homegrown kraut cabbage and apples.

Bill La Croix happened to be attending Marquette University during the same time I attended Spencerian. He and his wife lived in an apartment on the Marquette University campus, and I visited with them. It felt great to see Bill and his wife and to have friends in Milwaukee to talk to.

In October or November, Terry Dunlavy asked to sleep over a couple nights. A family member was getting married in Milwaukee, and he didn't want to stay at a motel. The ladies were delighted. They set up a bed on a chaise in the living room. I picked up Terry at the bus depot when he arrived and took him back there when he left. I was invited to the wedding and reception. It was exciting to have Terry visit with me for a couple days and share experiences.

My course work at Spencerian included typewriting classes, spelling, and learning machine shorthand.

A court reporter's work consists of taking down what

is being said in shorthand and transcribing it into a written court report. Sometimes, the judge asks the court reporter to read back some of statements made during a trial. Shorthand, typing, and spelling were thereby the essentials for studying court reporting.

I received the best grades in typing I ever had. I was becoming more skilled in typing for transcription.

I aced spelling-- straight A's. We covered long words, difficult words, words used in courtroom language and courtroom drama. None of these words phased me. I scored 100's on all the spelling tests.

In order to learn machine shorthand the Spencerian student needed to purchase a stenotype machine with stand.

The user of the stenotype keyboard was able to be more proficient by using the keyboard on a stand instead on a table or desk.

The stenotype keyboard looked more like piano keys

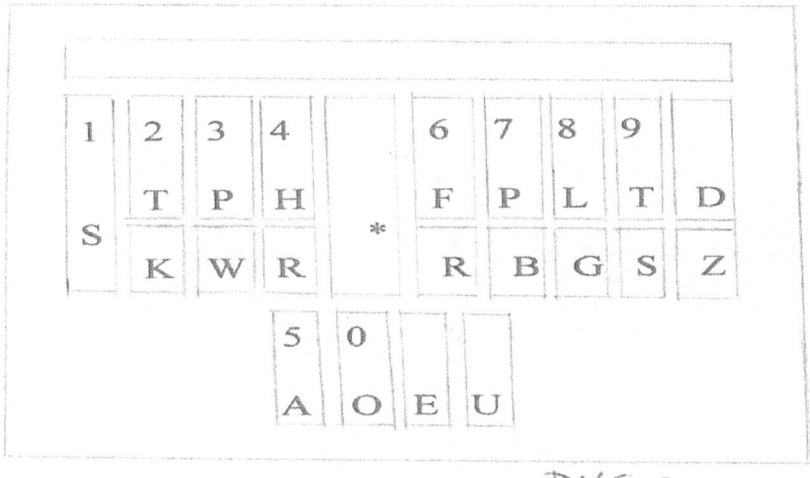

than typewriter keys and is often called a chorded keyboard. More than one key was able to be pressed at the same time. A single stroke created a word, unlike the typewriter stroke creating only one letter or number. Actually, we were creating sounds on paper instead of actual words.

The sounds printed out on a narrow paper strip with folds. There was no sound when you depressed the keys and printed on the paper.

Since the keyboard contained only 21 keys, it didn't include all vowels and consonants. The letters "C" and "I" were not on the keyboard. The letter "K" was used for the letter "C". Pressing letter keys and the number pad simultaneously produced numbers. We had to learn to press keys to write in phonetics.

We had to learn to press or type out at least 225 words per minute at high accuracy. Proficient users of this machine achieved up to 300 words per minute.

I took my stenotype machine home every night and practiced typing to increase my proficiency.

Many ways exist to combine letters to make different sounds. Each student or court reporter uses different theories in creating sounds. Each person develops personal shortcuts and different ways of writing. Even if most stenotypes write similar, most court reporters cannot read each other's work.

Some court reporters get so busy or follow such a tight schedule as to not have time to translate or edit their work into a transcribed court report. Then they use an assistant trained in phonetics, punctuation, and legal formatting to do this part of their work for them.

I performed with excellence in stenotype class. I was able to create most sounds or phonetics on the stenotype machine onto paper as spoken by the instructor. I excelled with ease in reading back what I created. I became one of the best translators in the class.

Nonetheless, I became stressed out with the actual preparation of the transcription into a finished report. I didn't, therefore, complete my studies for court reporting.

A business college was not on the same level as an academic college as far as qualifying a student to be in school to avoid the draft. Uncle Same was after me. It wasn't going to be long before I became drafted.

Actually, I wasn't trying to avoid serving my country in the Armed Forces. In fact, I was looking forward to it. Roger had served in the Navy and Donnie in the Army. My cousin Gary had served in the Army. He looked sharp in his uniform. Gary Korth had been serving in the military, too.

A couple guys from Shiocton, Bob Knoke and Bob Kelley, had talked about signing up for the buddy system. Doing the buddy system ensured you and your buddies stayed together at least through basic training.

I decided to go along with them on the buddy system, signing up for the early draft.

Part Two

I'm in the Army Now, 1962-1964

Fort Leonard Wood logo, Company A, 5th Battalion

Aerial view of Fort Leonard Wood

MEMORIES

I remember Fort Leonard Wood.
I remember getting the GI haircut.
I remember reveille.
I remember train fire with the M1 rifle.
I remember bivouac-- sleeping in a shelter tent, all wet and muddy.
I remember pulling guard duty.

The Missouri Ozarks

Uncle Sam sent three recruits from Shiocton to the Missouri Ozarks. Bob Kelley, Bob Knoke, and I arrived in Milwaukee on January 22, 1962 for our induction into the United States Army under the buddy system. The buddy system guaranteed keeping us together in the same unit.

Besides the clothes on our bodies, we each carried a small bag of personal items.

We rode on the Army bus from Milwaukee to Fort Leonard Wood, Missouri. We were assigned to Company A, 5th Battalion, 2nd Training Regiment for basic training. There were 414 in our Company A.

The name of the fort came from Major General Leonard Wood in honor of his action against the Apache Indian Geronimo. The fort had developed a reputation as one of the major installations for recruit basic training.

As soon as we departed the Army bus, we underwent medical exams, got the GI haircut, and picked up our Army supplies. Our supplies included sheets, pillow, wool Army blanket, combat boots, dress shoes, fatigues, dress uniform, caps, socks, and underwear. As we walked in a line and picked them up at a counter, we packed the items of issue into a large duffel bag. Each of us also received our own dog tags. The number on each soldier's tags identified him, and we had to memorize our ID number.

We carried our duffel bag and personal bag to our assigned barracks. We were allowed to choose our own bunk.

After we got settled in our barracks, we received platoon assignments. Soldiers perform effectively in small groups, i.e. patrols. Patrols were based on barracks assignments.

Our platoon sergeants and patrol leaders put out the rules and regulations right from the start. They repeated them and repeated them throughout our eight weeks of basic training.

Whenever a recruit encountered an officer, he had to salute him and say "Good morning, sir" or "Good afternoon, lieutenant." If you didn't salute, you got into deep trouble.

A bugle signal or whistle woke us up early in the morning. It meant we had to get ready for assembly. This was called reveille. We had to assemble outdoors in patrol formation. It was still dark outside, probably 6:00 a.m. Fatigue trousers, combat boots, and t-shirts were the norm for assembly, P.T. training, and some obstacle course training. We were allowed to tuck our cigarette packs in our t-shirt sleeves.

If a soldier didn't have his t-shirt tucked in his pants, his pants legs tucked in his boots, and his boots tied, he had to get down and do push-ups, at least 20, most often 50.

When smoking outdoors, you needed to pocket the papers and filters, leaving nothing on the ground from the cigarette, except ashes or loose tobacco.

After reveille, we had an hour to do some housekeeping chores. We needed to shave, wash (or shower), get dressed, make our bunks, tidy up our bunk and locker area, empty the gallon cans, sweep the barracks, and clean the latrine. Only six guys occupied the latrine at the same time. The rest worked on cleanup of the barracks and their bunk and locker area. As room became available in the latrine, the other guys went in to do their personal hygiene.

There was no modesty in the latrine or the barracks. The guys were half to full naked during this hour of cleanup after reveille.

A soldier was in for a bad time if he didn't do personal hygiene. He ended up getting dunked in the showers and being scrubbed with a hard brush. A couple guys in our unit ended up this way because they didn't clean themselves up.

We had to pass inspections. Our bunk had to be so tight as to be able to bounce a quarter on it. Our lockers had to be neat. The barracks floors had to be spotless and clean, including the stairs.

We needed to be trained in saluting as a first priority. Although it seemed to be a simple task, a few of us found it to be a difficult thing to do. Actually, we had to learn to do it in an acceptable and approved manner. If you did an improper salute, down you went for more push-ups.

The next training job for the recruit was learning how to use the M1 rifle and train fire.

We needed to learn how to handle the M1 rifle. We did this in dismounted drill exercises. We learned the proper way to carry a rifle. We learned how to hold the rifle in the positions of "attention" and "at ease."

Before going to the shooting range, we were instructed on how to assemble and disassemble our weapon, the M1 rifle.

We went to the shooting range every day until we became skilled in shooting. We didn't stop going to the range until we had at least earned a marksman badge. A marksman shoots well, making a number of hits in or near bull's-eye.

We shot at targets from assimilated fox holes and at the prostrate position.

We did one hour of physical training at least three days per week. We did push-ups, pull-ups, and sit-ups, plus some other exercises. We exercised with and without the M1 rifle.

We marched and marched and marched. We marched in the compound, a gravel covered surface. We marched the streets of the fort, all covered with asphalt. We marched with rifles and without rifles. Some marching tactics worked better without rifles, like the marching maneuver "to the rear march," when we spun completely around on our heels. We marched forward. We marched to the left. We marched to the right. Commands were shouted out, "To the left," "To the right," and "To the rear march." We marched at least an hour daily. Sometimes we marched and walked long distances for an hour or two. We sang cadences as we marched, and they went like this.

>Sound off
>1-2
>Sound off
>3-4
>Sound off
>1-2-3-4
>1-2------3-4

After each cadence, the guys made up their own corny, rhymed cadences, and they enjoyed doing them. The more they did them, the more hilariously funny they became. We practiced marching in review, saluting the reviewing stand in preparation for parades and graduation exercises.

Barracks lined the streets, with approximately 10 buildings on each side of the street per block. The barracks buildings were two-story buildings.

Bunk beds lined each side of the barracks rooms. Two clothes lockers occupied the space on the wall in between the bunk beds, and two foot lockers took up aisle space at the foot of the beds. Each soldier, of course, had a foot locker and a clothes locker.

Support poles lined each side of the aisle. On each pole hung a gallon tin can filled with water at least half way. The cans were our ash trays. When you smoked, you either stood by one of them or set one by you.

The officers' quarters and the latrine occupied one end of the barracks on each floor. The officers' quarters accommodated three officers, like non-commissioned staff sergeants, lieutenants, or captains. The latrine housed about six toilets, urinals, sinks, and showers. You didn't have any privacy in the latrine or in the barracks.

At the end of each day, we showered, cleaned up our area, cleaned our rifles, polished our brass belt buckles, and spit shined our boots. Lights were shut off early. If you didn't get done before the lights went out, you had to do it in the latrine. Boots had to be cleaned, polished, and spit shined by rubbing a water-soaked cotton ball in a circular motion on your boot until it shined.

Located near the barracks were the mess hall, the orderly room, the day room, the game room, and post exchange (PX). The orderly room, the day room, and the game room were all located in one building, but the mess hall and PX were in separate buildings. The fort also housed a main post exchange (main PX), a field house, and a post service club.

They trained us to overcome all sorts of obstacles. We had to climb up ropes, go over hurdles, and crawl through barrels or culverts. The culverts were empty but water-logged and mud-filled. We had to crawl under wire in mud and water. When we were crawling, we had to keep our elbows down and our rifles up to keep our rifles clean. Actually, we crawled on our elbows and knees. We also crawled on our backs with our rifles astride our chest and stomach.

We learned how to handle bayonets, survive gas attacks, and throw grenades.

Our Company issued each soldier in the unit a number of field gear items, namely: bayonet, grenades, shells, gas mask, canteen, helmut, shovel, backpack, wide web belt supported by suspenders, poncho, half a tent, field rations, and the M1 rifle.

Our training peaked during the seventh week. We left for bivouac on Monday morning and returned Friday evening. We marched to our training areas and got a good experience of being out in the open with only tents for shelter. It was rigorous even through assimilated.

We lived on field rations from our backpacks and on chow served by our Company cooks. We had tables and

benches to eat on, the standing room only kind, luxuries not normal in real combat. We were allowed to use Bunsen burners to heat our field rations. They tasted much better warmed up. In fact, we found it difficult to stomach them cold. Our rations included cans of meat and beans, meat and vegetable hash, and meat and vegetable stew.

    We had to endure periods of rainy downpours. We got wet and soaked and muddy, but the poncho helped to keep our drab olive fatigues dry.

    Since you only had half a tent, you bunked with a

Army shelter tent

buddy and made up a shelter tent. During periods of heavy rain, two soldier buddies set up their tent, crawled inside wet and muddy, and reclined as they were.

When not in use, we stacked our M1's pyramid style.

We underwent proficiency tests on grenade warfare, with rifle grenades and hand grenades, on gas warfare, and on

bayonet warfare. We marched doing squad tactics, practicing close combat.

Needless to say, we were happy soldiers on coming back to the barracks Friday evening. We were given the next day off just for cleanup and rifle cleaning.

We didn't do much more training after bivouac. We did primarily marching and inspections.

We all pulled guard duty and kitchen patrol (K.P.). A roster was posted, and we had to show for guard duty and K.P. when scheduled to do them.

K.P. was divided into several tasks. Some of us helped with food preparation, some in the serving line, and some in washing dishes. The dishwasher area got nicknamed the grease trap. I peeled carrots and potatoes and worked the grease trap.

When doing guard duty, we reported to the guard building. All the patrols took turns pulling guard duty. At least 16 soldiers guarded during a 24-hour shift. Eight guys slept as eight guarded. The changing of the guard occurred repeatedly throughout the night. The guards were trucked to their area of watch. Anyone attempting to cross a guarded area had to shout out a password to pass. I didn't encounter anyone trying to pass in my area of watch.

Payday occurred once a month. You stood in line for payroll until you reached the payroll table. You gave your name to the company clerk. The company clerk read off the amount of payment to the company officer. The company officer gave you the amount due in new, crisp bills. My payroll was $84 a month. This was good pay considering I had free room and board.

Opportunities arose throughout these weeks of basic training for me to get together with my buddies Bob Kelley and Bob Knoke. I developed new acquaintants, too. I had some new buddies, some in other barracks, other companies, about 56 guys total.

I didn't do much during the week in addition to training, personal hygiene, barracks cleanup, and cleanup of my bunk area. Perhaps, I found a few moments to spare to write a letter to my family at home in Shiocton. I made up for it on weekends.

I took full advantage of any free time given to me. I didn't stay in the barracks on weekends because if you stuck around you got put on extra duty. I visited all my buddies in the other barracks. Occasionally, a few of us had pizza and beer at the pizza place on base. The pizza tasted good and so did the beer, even if only 3.2%. There was no chance of getting drunk on the 3.2 even if you drank it all night. We also went to the post service club, drinking the 3.2 and shooting pool or playing some other game.

The USO Club was the popular place to go. USO was founded by President Franklin D. Roosevelt in the 1940s as a GI's home away from home. We went there to dance, to listen to music, and to watch movies. Hollywood celebrities came to the USO to entertain troops. More than 400,000 performances occurred at over 3,000 USO Clubs. Entertainers included Bing Crosby, Bob Hope, Judy Garland, Bette Davis, Frank Sinatra, Marlene Dietrich, the Andrews Sisters, Doris Day, and many more.

I went to the PX often. I went there at night to get something to snack on or drink. I spent more time there though on my days off. I discovered some neat looking sweaters at the PX, and I bought one. It was a hard choice because there so many beautiful ones to choose from. I didn't stop at just buying one sweater though. Every month I bought one until I had about six of them. I also discovered a nice selection of pillow shams at the PX. They were beautiful and many had poems to mother on them. I bought a few and sent them home to Ma. It was difficult to choose these, too, because they were all so beautiful as well.

Neither zip codes nor sales tax had any existence in 1962. It only cost me two four-cent stamps to send home a pillow sham.

The main PX was further from our barracks but had more to offer, including barber shops, gas stations, fast food bars, liquor stores, movie theaters, and vehicle repair shops.

Time marched along swiftly and soon we did the real parade in review and saluted a live reviewing stand. We graduated, said goodbye to our friends, and moved on to our new assignments. Kelley, Knoke, and I were assigned to the Mountain Post.

I enjoyed basic training for the most part. I liked marching, shooting the M1, shooting rifle grenades, and guard duty. We had gone through an intensive course of basic training. We acquired the basic "know how" of soldiering-- marching, shooting, fighting. We had proven ourselves. We had developed military skills and learned the importance of team play where others depend upon you, carrying these skills with us throughout our lives and careers.

I looked forward to my assignment at the Mountain Post.

Bob Kelley

Bob Knoke

Boone

Pike's Peak, as seen in the background from Colorado Springs, Colorado

The Mountain Post, Fort Carson, Colorado

The automatic rifle (AR)

MEMORIES

*I remember moving onto advanced training at Fort Carson.
I remember going home on vacation leave in April, 1962.
I remember visiting all the scenic places in Colorado.
I remember going home on leave in 1963.
I remember the day Kennedy was shot.
I remember going on a motorcade to the State of
      Washington for assimilated war tactics.
I remember using the library on military base.
I remember firing the coal furnaces on base.*

The Mountain Post

After graduating from basic training, Bob Knoke, Bob Kelley, and I moved onto advanced individual training with an active army unit at the Mountain Post, Fort Carson, Colorado.

Fort Carson was named in honor of Brigadier General Kit Carson. The post had the distinction of being one of the best installations for preparing soldiers to win on the battlefield.

I was assigned to Company C, 2nd Battalion, 61st Infantry. We became known as "Chargin' Charlie," best by test.

Fort Carson was located immediately south of Colorado Springs in El Paso County, Colorado. It was situated at a high altitude, one mile above sea level, with no humidity. Some guys fainted on their first exposure to the high altitude, but I had no problem with it.

Fort Carson and Colorado Springs were situated near Pike's Peak at the base of the most famous mountains of the United States, the eastern edge of the southern Rocky Mountains. The scenery was beautiful. As the sun rose each day the color on the side of the mountain was bright and beautiful pink. Now as I think of it, the color wasn't pink but actually a red or copper toned sandstone.

The company compound's surface consisted of fine gravel stone. With all of the foot traffic and some vehicular

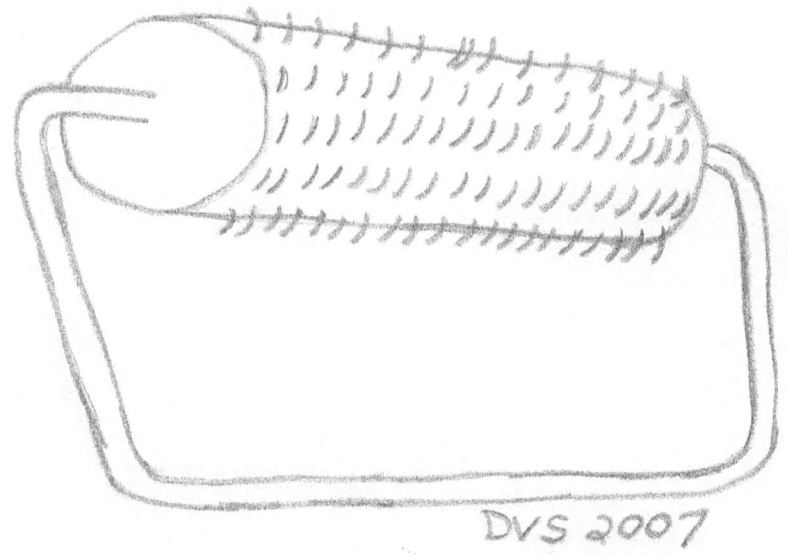

Company compound yard broom

traffic, the stones got roughened up. The surface was made smooth again by sweeping it with a pull broom. One or two guys pulled it. The broom was heavy enough to level out the stones as it was pulled across them back and forth across the compound, but the broom was not too heavy to pull. I got a thrill out of pulling the broom. It was satisfying to notice how neat the compound looked after being swept with the broom.

Once the compound's gravel was all swept with the broom, it was rolled.

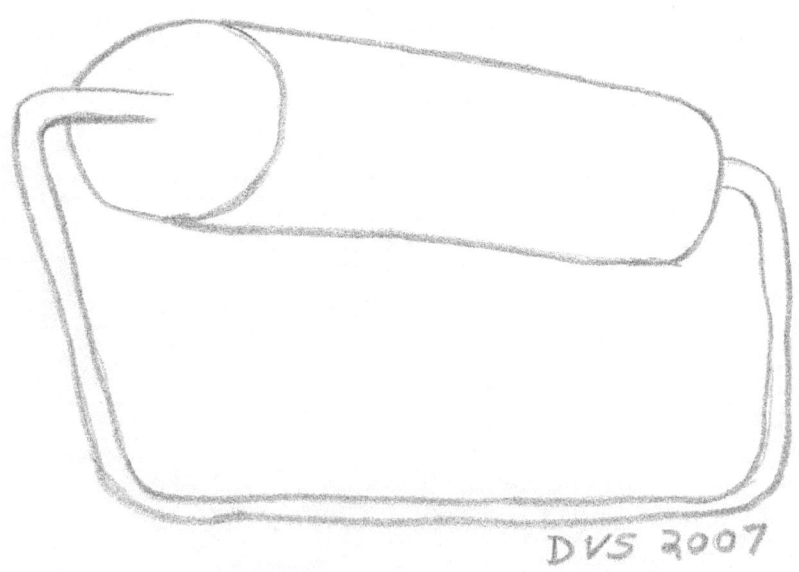

Company compound yard roller

      The life of the soldier at Fort Carson was similar to the one I had experienced at Fort Leonard Wood. We marched, exercised, and improved our skills in train fire shooting. We took turns performing guard duty and K.P. We had reveille, did personal hygiene, spit shined our boots, cleaned our barracks, and underwent inspections.

      We continued working on individual protective measures. We walked in an enclosure with our gas masks off, then the gas was turned on, our eyes began to burn, tears ran down our cheeks, and then we were allowed to put on our gas masks. Sometimes we walked in the enclosure with the gas already turned on and our gas masks on and then we had to take off our gas masks.

      We went to Army school. There were times when all we did was go to classes all day all week. Each man in the unit was issued a pocket handbook as a ready reference to general military subjects to ensure all proper procedures, reports, and orders were followed in all situations. The handbook was assembled to allow each man to add notes and make changes in it as needed. I added many notes as we attended classes.

The handbook was the size of a 4 x 6 inch card and grew to be an inch thick. Once we received the handbook and learned everything in it, we had to carry it on our person all the time and not part with it. We had to keep it dry, too, during those times of crawling in mud and water.

The subjects learned and contained in the handbook included: military courtesy and conduct, guard duty, protective measures, prisoner of war conduct, handling weapons (the M-1 rifle, the automatic rifle, the automatic .45 pistol, and the machine gun), map reading, first aid, combat training with bayonets and grenades, radio use, and the like.

Many dust storms occurred. Whenever there was a dust storm, we pulled extra guard duty, wearing face masks and safety glasses.

We also experienced many fierce wind storms, and once more we had to pull extra guard duty. The wind was so powerful you were unable to even walk a step forward.

Although Kelley, Knoke, and I were in different barracks and patrols, we continued to take advantage of opportunities to get together and share experiences. Knoke wanted to go to Germany, but he didn't convince Kelley and I to go along. In order to do active duty overseas, a soldier had to sign up for it before the end of his first year of draft because the duration of oversea duty needed to be at least two years. By the end of the year, Knoke had signed up for another year and parted company with us.

Knoke and I

When we were off duty, we had many opportunities for recreation at the PX, main PX, service club, and USO shows. I went to the PX and main PX most often. I bought more sweaters and filled my locker with them. I bought and sent home to Ma a few more pillow shams. It only cost me nine cents to send them from Colorado, a penny more than from Missouri. One of the shams was of Vermilion Bay, Ontario. I am sure Pa enjoyed looking at it because it was the place where Pa and Gerald hunted moose in Canada.

We were all given vacation leave to go home and visit

Enjoying vacation leave with Ma

our families. We signed up for it in the company office. I took my first vacation in April, 1962.

Enjoying vacation leave with Russell and Carl

Going home in April, 1962 and spending some time with the family was great, but I missed being there during the summer of 1962. Ma wrote and told me she harvested lots of strawberries in her berry patch. Aunt Edna even came up one day to help pick them.

Joyce, Aunt Edna, and Ma with berries

We also got weekend passes. When you took an excused leave or pass, you signed out in the company office when you left and signed in when you returned. You were allowed to go anywhere on the post though without a pass.

I used many excused passes to go off base. It was easy to go off base. City of Colorado Springs buses made regular stops on base.

I learned about traveling on my own. I knew nothing about public transportation. I traveled long distances by bus, by train, and by airplane. On my first trip home, April, 1962, I took the bus home and rode on the train on the way back. The train was faster than the bus, and I enjoyed the scenic view along the way. I traveled by air on my second trip home around Easter time in 1963.

Mary was confirmed at St. Denis in Shiocton in 1963.

Mary on Confirmation Day, 1963

Wearing my khaki uniform, 1963

    I visited many exciting places off base, like Colorado Springs, Pike's Peak, the Air Force Academy, the Garden of the Gods, the Royal Gorge, Seven Falls, and Cave of the Winds.

    Exploring Colorado Springs was delightful. Touring the city was big adventure for me, becoming acquainted with all the restaurants, bars, movie theaters, shops, and so forth. At first I went to Colorado Springs with some of the other guys. Once I learned how to get around, I went alone.

    If I stayed in Colorado Springs all weekend, I reserved a hotel room for two nights as soon as I got in town. I knew when I arrived in town how long I planned to stay.

The clothing stores attracted me because I was interested in civilian clothes to wear.

Before going home on vacation leave, I went to the bus depot and train station to get travel information.

The U.S. Air Force Academy trains and educates young men to be officers for the United States Air Force. Graduates receive a Bachelor of Science degree and a commission as second lieutenant. The Academy cadets must commit to serving a number of years in the U.S. Air Force after graduation.

The U.S. Air Force Academy attracts over a million

The Terrazzo

tourists each year. Tourists are attracted to the large, square pavilion known as the Terrazzo because of the walkways made of terrazzo tiles amid a checkerboard of marble strips. An "air gardens" section 700 feet long featured lighted pools and walkways. The Cadet Chapel is a symbol of the Academy. It

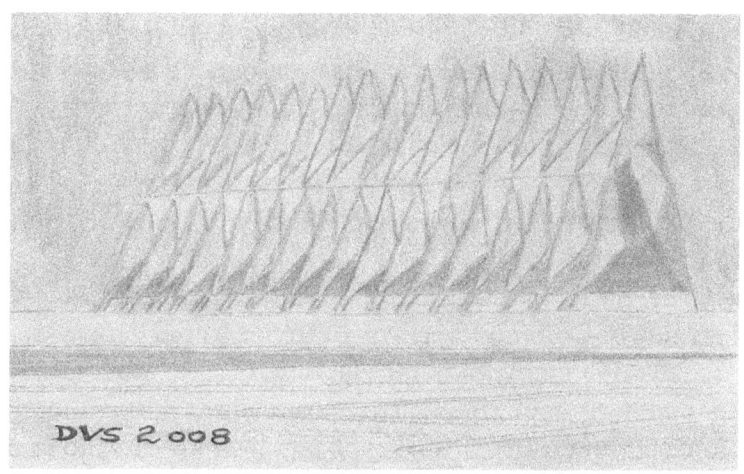

The Cadet Chapel's tetrahedrons

ranks as the most beautiful of all modern American academic architecture. One hundred identical aluminum tetrahedrons comprise the structure with colored glass in between them. It houses a 1,300-seat Protestant chapel, a 500-seat Catholic chapel, a 100-seat Jewish chapel, and interfaith rooms for services of other religions. My visit here was a marvel to behold. You have to see it and experience it to appreciate it.

Pike's Peak, a mountain 10 miles west of Colorado Springs, became famous because of races up the side of the mountain. It was named for explorer Zebulon Pike after he led an expedition in the area. The summit is surmounted by a cog railroad operating out of Manitou Springs and by automobile on the Pike's Peak Highway although half of the road was unpaved at this time. A popular hiking route called Barr Trail also provided access for walkers, hikers, and bikers to the summit. Stories of climbing the summit boast of dribbling a ball to the top and walking backwards to the top. A guy even pushed a peanut with his nose up the incline to summit in a period of three weeks. Actually, being at the top was uncomfortable because the air was so thin up there with only 60% of the available oxygen at sea level. There wasn't much to do up there either, with just a visitor's gift shop. The thrill of it all was ascending the Peak. Snow abounded on the Peak year round. Thunderstorms occurred throughout the summer with dangerous lightning, hail, and wind gusts over 100 miles per hour. It was probably the source of the heavy winds at Fort Carson. I witnessed a beautiful view of Pike's Peak below the summit.

The Garden of the Gods, a public park, was located in the confines of Colorado Springs. Entrance to the park was free. There were many trails for walking, hiking, mountain biking, and horseback riding. There were signs throughout the park to watch out for rattlesnakes. Visitors were allowed to do rock climbing on the unusual steep rock formations. It is noted for its outstanding geologic features with the ancient sedimentary beds of red and white sandstones and limestone tilted vertically. Legend says the name Colorado comes from the color of the sandstone. The colors of the sandstone were fantastic, just like the Rocky Mountain hillside seen from Fort Carson. Fossils abounded within the park. Hogbacks resembling the backs and spines of a pig consisted of layers of sandstone with tilted layers. A notable rock feature was called the Kissing Camels. It looked like two huge camels sitting face to face with their lips touching. Two other popular rock formations were Balanced Rock and the Siamese Twins.

Balanced Rock

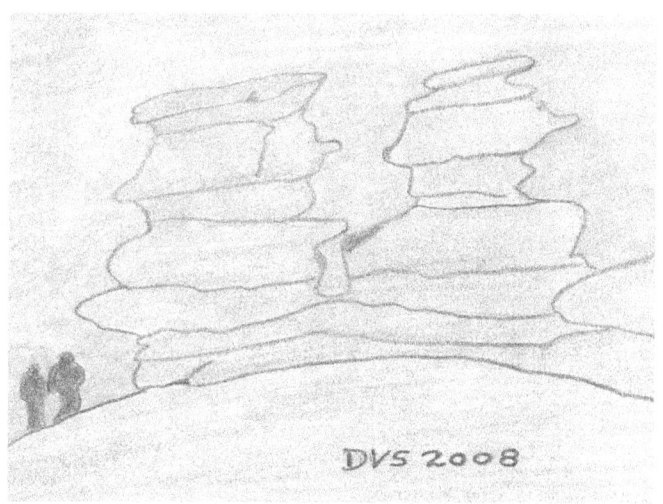
Siamese Twins

The Royal Gorge was awesome. It measured 50 feet wide at the base, a few hundred feet wide at the top, and 1,200 feet deep. The Gorge stretched 10 miles long. The Gorge

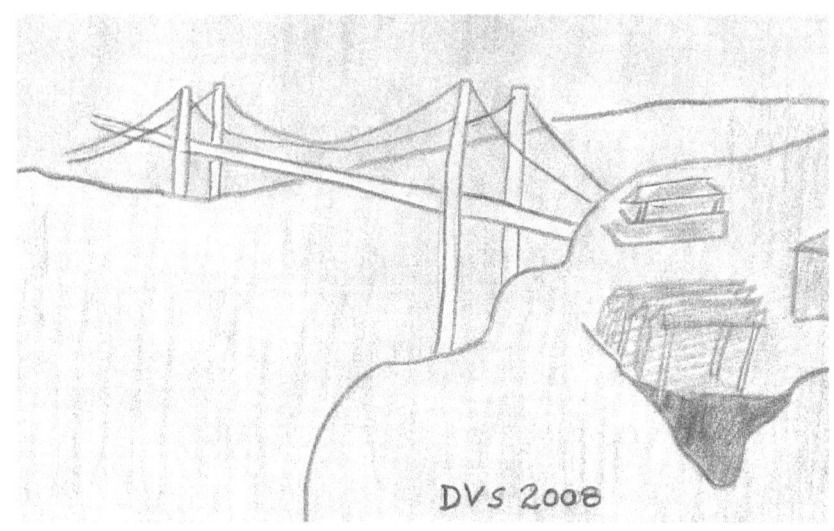

developed from long and direct erosion through hard rock. A bridge was built at 1,053 feet above the base and is known as the highest suspension bridge over water in the world. A train travels on a railroad at the base, and whitewater rafting occurs on the water way. Rock climbing and bungee jumping are permitted. It's scary standing on the suspension bridge, but the view is terrific. Everything down below looks so miniature. I visited the Royal Gorge many times.

Seven Falls is a series of seven cascading waterfalls, reaching a height of 181 feet. Visitors needed to climb 224 steps to get to the top.

The cave of the Winds is located just west of Colorado Springs near the Manitou Cliff Dwellings.

I wrote letters home all the time and received letters from home as well. The letters served to keep everyone informed about what was happening, plus it was exciting to have your name called off at mail call, meaning you had gotten a letter or package. A lonely GI enjoys getting a letter.

The year was 1963, and Mary and Karen had entered high school. Ma now helped harvest cabbage in the fall, alongside Pa, Carl, Alice, Lennie, and Mary.

Ma, Alice, and Carl cutting cabbage

Alice, Carl, Ma, and Lennie loading cabbage

Russell had a whim to occasionally ride the painted pony.

**Russell riding the pony by Carl's kids,
David, Darrell, Duane**

Most of the Army chow tasted ok. The exceptions were the eggs sunny side up and turkey. I had a difficult time with those soft eggs. It was nothing but hard fried eggs for me from then on. The turkey didn't seem to be cooked long enough. Some parts of it were tough.

We celebrated Thanksgiving and Christmas on base as much as civilians did. Our meals included turkey, ham, and chicken, along with potatoes, dressing, gravy, carrots, jello, cakes, and ice cream. On these days the soldier needed to wear his full dress uniform at mealtime. We all got passes unless we were scheduled for K.P. I enjoyed receiving a box of cookies and candy from home. I shared these with my buddies. We all shared our goodies sent from home. These were hard days to get through without family. I suffered through these two holidays during the years of 1962 and 1963 without family close by. My buddies were my family back then. At night on those special days I went into Colorado Springs and went to the movies.

On one weekend pass, my buddies and I took a trip to the Mile High City, Denver, Colorado, and slept over one night at a hotel. We dined at a couple fine restaurants. Denver is the state's capital, and we caught several glimpses of the gold-domed capitol building on our rides on the city buses during our stay. We took an opportunity to ride the many bike trails in the Denver area. We toured some of the parks. Denver has over 200 of them. Some of us kayaked the white water of the Platte River at Confluence Park. Golf courses, recreation centers, museums, and girlie shows. A concert under the stars was seen at the Red Rocks Amphitheatre.

On some nights on weekends, the guys in our barracks patrol just sat around in their underwear in the barracks on their foot lockers, drinking booze and telling jokes and stories.

Barracks buddies, Weeks, Pittman, Waite, Gardner, Ruby, Franks

One night one of my barracks buddies got drunk and threw up all over the latrine area. Who got to clean it up? Boone, of course. Nobody else happened to be around at the precise moment.

Some of my the guys at Fort Carson, like Folmar and Gavette, had their own jalopies.

Folmar and Gavette cleaning jalopy

The day John Kennedy was assassinated, I was pulling K.P. duty. We all stopped our work, went outside, stood in awe, and went through a moment of silence. Soon afterwards, the fort went into alert. Guard duty shifts started and continued until the Nation was once more made secure under President Lyndon Baines Johnson. We went into alert once again when Dr. Martin Luther King Jr. and Attorney General Robert Kennedy were shot.

We played war games and went on military maneuvers.

We all went to the military football games on base. As a form of recreation during the half time, some of us got a chance to play war games. We even used a horse to help lift up a dummy of a player of the opposing military team and hang him in effigy.

"Get him"

"Hang him in effigy"

Boone, Forsythe, Ruby

On our first military maneuver, we motorcaded from Fort Carson to the State of Washington. We rode in canvas-covered Army trucks with seating on both sides.

We made regular stops to eat chow and make pit stops. We made comfort stations at our stops by digging shallow pits and placing wooden structures over them, filling the pits with dirt on departure. We often ate field rations in the truck, using Bunsen burners to heat them up.

The dirt roads were dry and dusty.

We set up tents each night for sleeping. Instead of setting up shelter tents, we used larger canvas tents capable of housing a group of soldiers.

I became constipated on about the second day of the maneuver. I went on sick call and took some laxatives. The laxatives cured my constipation.

Upon arrival at Washington State, the war tactics began. Chargin' Charlie assaulted a huge mountain. I got winded on the ascent of the mountain. We fired rifle grenades, threw hand grenades, engaged in close combat and gas warfare, and overcame obstacles.

Our unit captain, Captain Charles Thoma, gave us haircuts on field maneuvers.

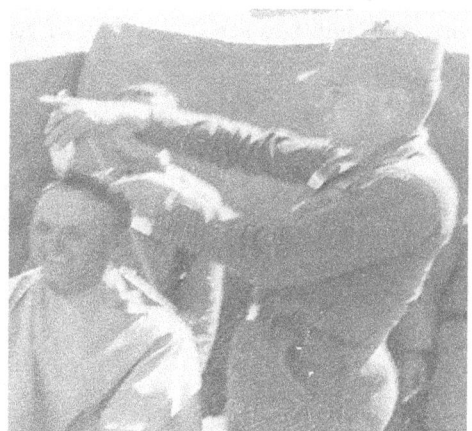

Captain Thoma gives me a GI haircut

We had a chance for church in the field, too. We had

an opportunity for confession, communion, and worship in the field. Confession in the field was actually embarrassing. I was accustomed to going to confession in the confessional, but in the field confession was face to face in the open. Just imagine, confessing your sins to a priest with no screen between us.

For another field maneuver, we were airlifted on Army cargo planes to the State of Georgia. Army trucks were secured to the center of the plane with cables, and we sat on seats on each side of the aircraft. Riding in a cargo plane felt weird.

I used the military library on base a few times. I loved the library. I became familiar with the parts of the library. I thought about librarianship as a profession. The idea of working in a library intrigued me. I wasn't going to be a teacher, artist; or a court reporter, but what about being a librarian. I loved books and reading. The more I thought about it, the more convinced I became this was what I was meant to be-- a librarian.

The American soldier got inoculated at regular intervals. Some of the shots were administered by needle and several by the needle gun. The needle gun was pushed up against your arm and zap the injection was in your arm. I kind of liked getting zapped with a shot more than the needle injection. We walked in a line through the injection station, getting one shot after another. We needed to exercise our arms for a short time afterwards to prevent getting a sore arm. Sometimes the pain from shots hurt so much some of us bawled like a baby.

We did mountain climbing training for a couple weeks and had fun doing it. We did this training in winter, sleeping in large canvas tents with cold weather sleeping bags and a stove in the middle of the tent for warmth.

We worked with ropes to traverse obstacles in most of these mountain climbing exercises. We wore a climbing harness most of the time. The harness had a belt, shoulder straps, and leg loops. We attached carabiners to the harnesses.

Carabiners were solid aluminum rings with a snap link to fasten to a rope. We walked on ropes across ravines with the carabiners attached to our harnesses. We attached our carabiners to a rope at a high point, sliding down to a low point. The one I had the most fun with was rappelling down the sheer face of a cliff by means of a double rope. I learned to do this well enough without skinning my knees. It felt good to be bouncing back and forth against the side of the cliff as I descended it.

    We learned to call our rifle a rifle and not a gun. We were told what our rifle was and what our gun was. If an infantryman called his rifle a gun, he had to pay for the consequence. Down for 50 push-ups.

    My platoon sergeant was a sharp-looking soldier, always dressed in clean khakis and spit-shined boots. He performed well in keeping the soldiers in his platoon in tip-top shape and doing the right things. One day though he made a big mistake. We were drilling on assimilated firing of our rifles with blanks. For some odd reason, when we were at rest, he began tapping the butt of his rifle on the ground with his hand over the end of the barrel. Low and behold, his rifle fired and his hand got all banged up.

    During the winter of 1964 an opportunity arose for me to be a fireman for Chargin' Charlie, and I took advantage of it. Three soldiers from our company were needed to do this job.

    Heat in the Army buildings came from coal furnaces. Coal had to be added to each furnace once per hour. It took an hour for a fireman to make his rounds of feeding coal to each furnace of each building. The fireman's schedule consisted of working eight hours, sleeping eight hours, and having eight hours of free time. Firemen were exempt from inspections because of the dirty work.

    A fireman went into the furnace room, added coal, and then rested and warmed up before going on to the next furnace room. A fireman had to be cautious during the resting and warm-up time, though, to not fall asleep. One of the firemen did indeed sleep on the job and got razzed about it.

When our unit's tour of duty ended, I was asked to stay on for an extra few months until a new fireman became available, and I accepted.

When I became ready for discharge, I had to go around with my discharge papers and get signatures from various personnel.

I packed and boxed up all my clothes and personal belongings and sent them home. We were allowed to take all of our Army clothes and paraphernalia along home. I saved and still have after all these years-- my dress uniform, some uniform pins, duffel bag, and pocket handbook. I wore my field boots and dress shoes as long as possible. I have used my duffel bag on many occasions.

Bob Knoke married my cousin Carol Minlschmidt. Bob Kelley married, too, and then he became blind and committed suicide because of it.

I learned how to be a man. I learned respect for authority. I learned a credo for life…always try to do your very best. I learned the code of conduct of the American soldier. We memorized it, and it became a part of us, never to be forgotten for the rest of our lives. "I will never forget that I am an American fighting man, responsible for my actions, and dedicated to the principles which made my country free. I will trust in my God and in the United States of America."

Pa (March, 1964), a month before my discharge

Part Three

Back in Titans Land, 1965-1967

MEMORIES

I remember being released from active duty at Fort Carson on my 25th birthday.
I remember collecting unemployment after my military discharge.
I remember working at a Neenah paper mill.
I remember working for Gug at the Van Straten Oil Company.

Back Home

    I didn't have a chance to go home during Easter this year because Easter Sunday was March 29, and Easter was too close to the time of my departure from active service at Fort Carson. I was busy packing and planning for my trip home then. Ma and my sisters Joyce, Alice, Karen, and Mary wore some nice looking Easter outfits in 1964. I saw their

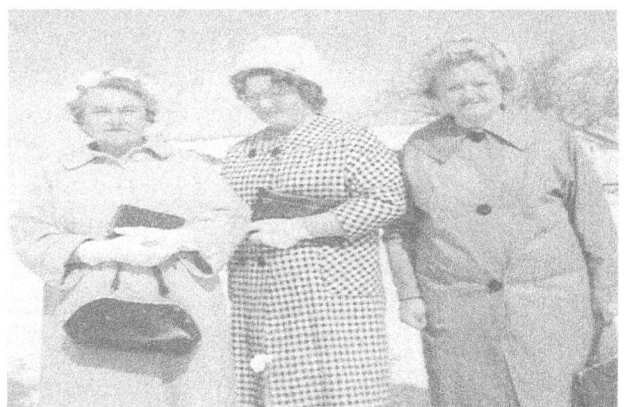

Ma, Mary, and Alice on Easter Sunday, 1964

Joyce, Karen, Lennie, Mary, Alice, and Ma on Easter Sunday, 1964

outfits after I came home. They always wore them for at least a month after Easter.

    I left Fort Carson early in the morning on April 16, 1964. I took a city bus to the airport, flew to Chicago's O'Hare Airport, connected to the Greyhound Depot, and rode a bus to Appleton, WI. Carl picked me up at the bus depot. It was my 25th birthday, and we arrived home in time to celebrate my birthday with cake and ice cream.

    I applied for unemployment compensation at the Appleton office of the Wisconsin State Unemployment Compensation Dept. My compensation request was approved. I was able to report to the New London office as well and went there most of the time. I had to report in each week to check for jobs. I collected $57.61 for 18 weeks, mid-April to mid-September, 1964.

Boone and the green apple (Summer, 1964)

As you most ably notice, Dear Reader, I still had a strong tie yet to green apples and continued to partake of opportunities to eat them.

A job opportunity surfaced in September, 1964 at a Neenah paper mill, and I enjoyed working there. I operated a machine spinning wide sheets of paper on a huge roll. As the roll became full, we sealed it, moved it aside, and started a new roll.

I used the money earned at the mill to pay off my Knights Templar loan. I saved the rest of my earnings and deposited them in a savings account I set up at the Shiocton Bank.

My employment at the mill only lasted a few months, September, 1964 to January, 1965, before I was laid off. I collected unemployment again from mid-January to mid-April, 1965.

Karen graduated from Shiocton High School in May, 1966.

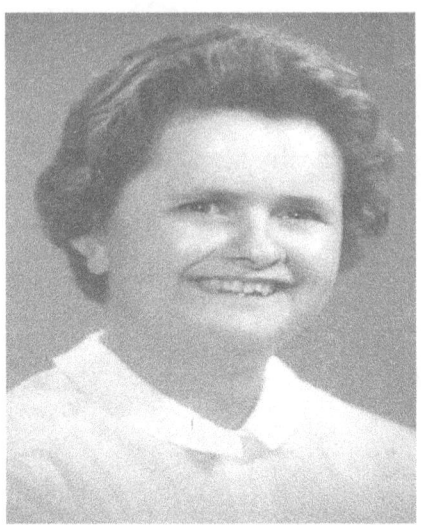

Karen, a Shiocton High School graduate, 1966
Picture Courtesy of F.J. Pechman

Joyce worked at one baby-sitting job after another. Most of the time she took care of cousin Tom's and his wife Janice's kids.

Joyce

During the periods of collecting unemployment, I made plans to return to college. I checked with my college adviser about continuing my education at OSC. When I left OSC in 1961, I was classified as a junior, and I had failed three courses. My adviser said I needed to take a couple off-campus courses transferable to OSC and get a B average in them.

I did exactly what my adviser asked me to do. I took two University of Wisconsin extension classes in the Fox Valley during the summer of 1965, evening courses, English 211 and Sociology 102, three credits each. Being back in school excited me and so did these courses. The Sociology course, namely The Sociology of Deviant Behavior, invigorated me. I learned a great deal about deviant behavior. I earned a B in each course, thereby obtaining the needed B average. Both courses transferred to OSC and counted towards my required course load requirement. I was readmitted to OSC and registered for the second semester of the 1965-1966 college year, beginning January, 1966.

Boone planting cabbage (Summer, 1964)

During the periods of unemployment, I helped out with growing and harvesting cabbage on the farm. The work was the same as before, sow seeds, pull and sort plants, work the land, plant, hoe, cultivate, spray, and harvest. I worked along with Carl, Lennie, Ma, Alice, and Mary. Pa helped if he was home, but he was busy at this time of his life going on fishing and hunting trips to Canada.

Pa and Carl were now partners in growing cabbage. They were partners in this business for 10 years. Pa and Gerald were also partners for a number of years raising whiteface Herefords.

Carl offered me the profits from six acres of cabbage as a wage for working on the farm in the fall of 1965. I had more jobs to perform to earn these profits, including plowing, cultivating, and spraying. I decided to do it because it was an opportunity to earn money for the next year of attending college.

Planting cabbage had become easier with a new piece of equipment Carl purchased. It was so easy Carl's young boys were able to do it. The seats on the new planter were up higher, and the boys just had to lay the plants on kind of a

The new cabbage planter at work

conveyer belt. They took turns putting plants on the conveyer belt.

Sometimes we loaded kraut onto a semi trailer.

Lennie, David, Carl, Dean, and the truck driver on break from loading a semi trailer with kraut

Sometimes our cabbage truck was unable to make it on its own, and the tractor needed to help pull it.

Lennie and Carl pulling out another truckload of kraut

Gerald, aka "Gug"

I also worked for Gerald at the Van Straten Oil Company. Gary "Beaver" Lemere and cousin Mark Brownson also worked for Gerald. When Gerald ventured off on his fishing and hunting trips to Canada and when he worked on his ice business, we worked many extra hours.

Gerald's station had four gas pumps, all full service stations. When a customer stopped at the pumps, we pumped the amount of gas they ordered. They either said, "Fill it up" or "Put in $5 worth." We asked if the oil needed to be checked and also washed the windshield.

Occasionally, a customer asked to have a lube job (oil change and grease job) but most had this done at Sielaff's garage, Don Little's, or Elmer Johnson's. A few, however, did their own lube jobs. Carl did his own. Mark, Beaver, and I did our own. It was cheaper to do it yourself.

Gerald did a big tire business, too. He had a big rack to house the tires. He sold new and used tires. He sent some tires to a tire company to be retread. He repaired tires, too. Gerald trained Mark, Beaver, and I on tire repair. He had a special apparatus for working on tires. I didn't perform well at this type of work in the beginning but gradually improved. When there was a lot of tire work needing to be done, two of us worked at the same time, one working on the tires and one tending the pumps.

I enjoyed working at the station during the pike run. Gerald had us open up the station during those times at 4:00 a.m. It seems crazy, but I loved opening up the station and working those early morning hours.

I fished on the Wolf, too. I liked fishing all night on Pa's or Roger's raft on the fisherman's bend, Bamboo Bend. It was a thrill to watch a fisherman yank a sturgeon out of the water and throw it in the trunk of his car right after the game wardens had driven by.

Gerald sold Christmas trees, too. I didn't have much to do with this, except to take the money when someone purchased a tree.

Owning a car meant car troubles. I took my car to Sielaff's, Don Little's, or Elmer Johnson's for repair on several occasions. Pa or Carl took our tractors down to Don Little's or Frank Shier's for repair.

Sometimes my car didn't start. Then we had to get out a chain and pull it with another car to get it started. Carl and I did it many times. We pulled until we were going about 30 miles per hour and tried to start it. It usually worked.

Most drivers used snow tires because they had better traction on the snow. Mud tires worked good, too, because their chunky tread patterns pulled well on muddy surfaces.

The snow tire orders at Gerald's station started coming in during November or December depending on the snow conditions.

Studded tires and tire chains had ceased to be a trade item. Studded tires had provided good traction on ice and tire chains did well on snow and ice, but their use became prohibited because of their damage to the asphalt roads.

There was some talk about sauerkraut being a miracle food or health food. Studies have claimed sauerkraut fights off the flu and prevents some kinds of cancer. Sauerkraut does contain vitamins C and K and is high in antioxidants, this we know. Fremont Company, makers of Frank's Quality Kraut, reported an increase in the product when reports surfaced of its success overcoming the flu. Ryan Downs, co-owner of the Great Lakes Kraut Company, Bear Creek, WI, became happy with the sales boost of kraut but took lightly the claims of it overcoming the flu. Ryan is married to my cousin Mary Miller (Aunt Grace's daughter). Ryan's company produces as much as 175,000 tons of canned, jar, and bagged kraut at its Bear Creek plant and other plants.

Some people make their own sauerkraut because they think the store brands are too sour and acidic.

MEMORIES

I remember celebrating Thanksgiving and Christmas.
I remember the traditions of Christmastime.

Sinterklaas

Tradition played an important role in the holiday celebrations of Thanksgiving and Christmas.

The kitchen was always a busy place, especially during the holidays. We all congregated in or near the kitchen until it became too crowded for Ma to get her work done and then Ma chased us all out.

Russell carved the Thanksgiving turkey, and I was thrilled to prepare the riced potatoes, also known as worm bug potatoes. Dressing, cranberries, gravy, homemade buns, jellos, and pies with whipped cream comprised the rest of the menu. The porch housed most all of the jellos and pies because there wasn't enough room in the refrigerator. Ma made her own whipped cream.

On Christmas Eve after Midnight Mass we had a light lunch of sandwiches made with homemade buns, plus raisin breads, banana breads, nut breads, and candied fruit cake.

On Christmas Day we had a light lunch similar to the Christmas Eve lunch, and we had a big supper. The evening meal consisted of beef or ham, white Navy baked beans, homemade buns, specialty breads, peanut cake, date bars, candied fruit cake, cookies, and candy.

We played cards after the big feed. Red Dog, Michigan Rummy, and Rummy were favorites.

Christmas was a beautiful time of the year with all the ornaments, balls, sparkling lights, and tinsel on the Christmas tree. The poinsettia was popular plant, originating from Mexico. Another popular item were candy canes. Candy canes, first used in Germany, were straight at first, but later they took on a curved shape, resembling a shepherd's staff.

Christmas music by all the popular artists, including Bing Crosby, Elvis Presley, and Rosemary Clooney, filled us with the Christmas spirit. Bing Crosby's "White Christmas" was a favorite. Young people sang or listened to all the Santa Claus songs.

The tradition of exchanging Christmas cards was a Victorian creation first introduced in Great Britain. The first Christmas cards included a family scene and the words "A Merry Christmas and a Happy New year to You."

Giving and receiving gifts was an important part of Christmas. We all looked forward with eager anticipation to receiving gifts from Santa Claus.

Holland is credited with the origination of Santa Claus. Children placed wooden shoes by the hearth on December 5th. The shoes were filled with straw for the white horse carrying the gifts and with food for St. Nicholas. This custom came to the United States with the Dutch colony of New Amsterdam and later evolved into hanging stockings at the fireplace, although the wooden shoes are still used in Dutch communities.

The Germanic celebrations of the Christmas ham, Yule logs, and the Christmas tree have continued to be celebrated into modern times.

St. Nicholas was first called Sinterklaas in the Netherlands. Sinterklaas and St. Nicholas later became known as Santa Claus. Santa Claus also became known as Father Christmas, Kris Kringle, or just simply Santa. He was and continues to be depicted as a fat, jolly man wearing a red coat and trousers with white cuffs and collar, a wide black leather belt, black boots, white hair, and a thick white beard, bringing gifts on December 6, Christmas Eve, or Christmas Day.

The Netherlands folklore of St. Nicolas symbolizes with the Germanic mythology, especially with the god Odin. Included in this folklore are the beard, hat and spear (staff), and the cloth bag used by the servants to capture naughty children. St. Nicolas and Odin rode white horses flying through the air. St. Nicolas was helped by a group of Zwarte Pieten, similar to elves.

One legend said Santa lived in the far north. American legend says he lives at the North Pole. Father Christmas resided in Finland. Other legends claim there is a Mrs. Claus living with him and elves making the toys and he makes a list of children, delivering presents to all the good boys and girls in the world and coal or sticks to the naughty children, all in one night. Legend further says Santa has flying reindeer, pulling his sleigh full of presents. In his poem "A Visit From St. Nicholas," known today as "The Night Before Christmas," Clement Clarke Moore depicts Santa as a heavyset person with eight reindeer named Dasher, Dancer, Prancer, Vixen, Comet, Cupid, Donder, and Blitzen.

Throughout the years many stories were made up by parents to keep the belief in St. Nicolas alive and to discourage misbehavior. There has always been opposition to teaching children to believe in Santa Claus. Those opposing the belief in Santa Claus reason it takes away the real religious or Christian purpose of Christmas and commercializes Christmas and you should put the birth of Jesus Christ in Christmas.

A Scattering of Dutch Sayings

De appel valt niet ver van de boom.
The apple never falls far from the tree.

Een kamer met boeken is redelijk gezel schap.
A room full of books makes sensible company.

Eendracht maakt macht.
United we stand, divided we fall.

Maak geen slapende honden wakker.
Let sleeping dogs lie.

Oude honden leren moeilijk pootjes geven.
You cannot teach an old dog new tricks.

In de oorlog en in de liefde is alles geoorloofd.
All is fair in love and war.

Als de ploeg werkt, dan blinkt hij.
The plow that works, shines.

Een os en een ezel span je beter niet voor dezelfde ploeg.
An ox and an ass don't yoke well to the same plow.

Vroeg d'r in, vroeg d'r uit, Werk als een hond en ga vooruit.
Early to bed, early to rise, Work like a dog and advertise.

Doe je best, God loet de rest.
Do your best, God does the rest.

De kleren maken de man.
Clothes make the man.

Haast en spoed is zelden goed.
Haste makes waste.

Leven en lafen leven.
Live and let live.

Proverbs of Other Lands

The Dutch traveler on the sea came upon many a proverb or saying and passed them along. Many proverbs, originally Dutch, became English proverbs.

I heard many of these sayings as I grew up. Even children repeated them. We said many of them as we walked the sidewalks to and from school.

Actions speak louder than words.

Adversity makes strange bedfellows.

After a storm comes a calm.

An apple a day keeps the doctor away.

April showers bring May flowers.

A barking dog never bites.

Beauty is only skin-deep.

Beggars can't be choosers.

The best things come in small packages.

The best things in life are free.

Better to be safe than sorry.

Better late than never.

'Tis better to have loved and lost than never to have loved at all.

Birds of a feather flock together.

You can't judge a book by its cover.

Never send a boy to do a man's job.

Business before pleasure.

When the cat's away, the mice will play.

A chain is only as strong as its weakest link.

A chain is no stronger than its weakest link.

Children should be seen and not heard.

Every cloud has a silver lining.

A man is known by the company he keeps.

Confession is good for the soul. (Scottish origin)

Don't count your chickens before they are hatched.

It is no use crying over spilt milk.

Curiosity killed the cat.

Do unto others as you would have others do unto you.

Early to bed and early to rise (makes a man healthy, wealthy, and wise).

Easy come, easy go.

Easy does it.

We must eat a peck of dirt before we die.

To err is human (to forgive divine). (Dutch origin)

Every man for himself.

Every man has his price.

Every man to his taste.

There is an exception to every rule.

Fact is stranger than fiction.

The family that prays together stays together.

First come, first served.

Fools rush in where angels fear to tread.

Garbage in, garbage out.

Never look a gift horse in the mouth.

God helps them (those) that help themselves.

What goes around comes around.

One good turn deserves another.

You cannot have your cake and eat it too.

Home is where the heart is.

Honesty is the best policy.

Hope springs eternal.

You can take a horse to the water, but can't make him drink.

What you don't know can't hurt you.

Knowledge is power.

Lightning never strikes the same place twice.

He who lives by the sword dies by the sword.

One man's loss is another man's gain.

Love is blind.

Make hay when the sun shines.

Man cannot live by bread alone.

Many are called but few are chosen.

The more the merrier.

Like father, like son.

Like mother, like daughter.

Nothing ventured, nothing gained.

Old soldiers never die.

Patience is a virtue.

Every picture tells a story.

There's no place like home.

If you play with fire, you get burnt.

Practice makes perfect.

Practice what you preach.

See no evil, hear no evil, speak no evil.

If the shoe fits, wear it.

Something is better than nothing. (German origin)

Spare the rod and spoil the child.

If at first you don't succeed, try, try, try again.

There is a time and place for everything.

Time is a great healer.

Truth is stranger than fiction.

It takes two to tango.

The way to a man's heart is through his stomach.

All's well that ends well.

Where there's a will, there's a way.

A woman's work is never done.

Life begins at forty.

Sticks and stones may break my bones, but words will never hurt me.

Step on a crack and you'll break your mother's back.

You are not worth your salt.

You are not worth a damn.

You are not worth a dime.

Your are not worth your wages.

You will not amount to a hill of beans.

MEMORIES

I remember hunting ducks.
I remember the first years of deer hunting.
I remember the days of fox hunting by Gug and others.

After the Wildlife

I hunted squirrel with cousins John and Joe during my high school years. I took my squirrel game home, dressed them, skinned them, and Ma cooked them for us. They tasted good.

After returning to civilian life, I didn't hunt squirrel anymore. Hunting squirrel wasn't a thrill for me any longer at the age of 25 and 26.

My hunting endeavors turned to ducks. Everybody was hunting ducks. We hunted off the Koepke Road. We hunted the dike by Harold's in the Black Slough. We hunted in the Wildlife Refuge on County Trunk M across from Pa's land. We hunted swamps, rivers, and waterways in the region.

I bought my hunting supplies from Ed Beyer's shop located behind Gerald's filling station and from Elmer Johnson's.

I bought my duck hunting trousers, jacket, cap, and boots in New London. Their color was tan, and they were guaranteed to keep me warm and dry. I was fond of my jacket with its big pockets and waterproof lining, providing room to actually carry ducks inside it. I never put any ducks in my jacket though. I still have the jacket to this day even though it doesn't fit. I guess it's just a keepsake, a reminder of happy days gone by.

Carl, Russell, and my cousins Tom, Dick, John, and

Joe all hunted ducks all over the Town of Bovina region. Carl, Russell, and Tom often got their daily game limit.

I hunted along the Koepke Road and in the Wildlife Refuge on County Trunk M.

My biggest thrill happened one day as I hunted in the Wildlife Refuge. Two beautiful blue-winged teal flew from the north around me and over me. Just as they passed above me, I shot, and they both fell. Wow! Two teal with one shot. I lucked out, too, because they fell on land, not in the water, a short distance from me. I didn't have a dog to fetch them if they had fallen in the water. They were beautiful birds. No duck hunting experience ever felt so good as this one.

My friend Dewey Wheeler and I became close duck hunting buddies. He picked me up every morning during the duck season. We hunted in the Wildlife Refuge without blind or hunting dog. There was a large pond in the refuge surrounded by a ridge overgrown with tall grasses and cattails. We sat in the grasses on the ridge, sometimes side-by-side, sometimes far apart. We had loads of fun hunting and talking at the refuge.

The Wheeler's lived off of State Hwy 54 across the road from Uncle Clark's farm house. I went down to the Wheeler's often. Dewey and his sisters Karen and Pat lived there with their mother. Dewey later married Beaver Lemere's sister Nancy.

I also hunted ducks on our farmland out behind the barn. Small pools of water formed during rainy periods, and ducks congregated at them. It was difficult to get close enough for a good shot at them though because there wasn't any tall grass to use as a blind. If they got near a corn field though, I was able to get off a shot at them.

Pa started hunting the white-tailed deer in 1926 when he was 25 years old. He got a monster of a buck on his first hunt at 310 Mercer, WI. A hunting crew of 10-16 men from Shiocton bought and owned a 40-acre plot in Mercer and built a shanty. Pa hunted there for 30 years. Pa loved to take off for

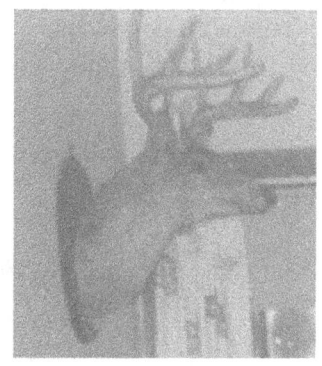 

Pa's big buck, 1926   **Nylands Shanty, Mercer, 1926**

the north to hunt 10 days. They hunted, did camp shores, and played cards at night. They took two weeks supplies and moved back in the bush. They hired a truck with a heater to keep warm.

No deer were sighted in Shiocton until 1940 and no hunting season until the 1950's. They started hunting in Shiocton in 1956. No land was posted. Hunters drove the woods all around the Town of Bovina. Lennie and I went with Pa and drove the woods for him.

Eventually hunting occurred on Pa's land on M. Hunting wasn't allowed during the fall until Pa and Gerald had moved their whiteface Herefords back to the farm. Hunting drives were made to move the deer. After a few years there were too many hunters and then hunting was permitted by Pa's family only.

There were no stands for hunting. Pa had a ladder to sit on. He allowed me to sit on it a few times. I scouted different spots but didn't see any deer.

Dewey's dad Bud just sat on the ground against a tree near a deer trail. He got a deer every year.

Gug, John Carpenter, and a few other hunters got a thrill out of hunting fox. After the deer season, they got after the fox. I heard the fox hunters on the walkie-talkie system in Gug's station when I was working there. They stopped at the station with their limit when done hunting for the day. They earned $5 per fox pelt.

MEMORIES

I remember going to the Packer games during the Lombardi years.
I remember some great Packer historical victories in the sixties.
I remember the Packers winning the Super Bowl two years in a row.

Go Pack, Go!

Cheering on the green and the gold!

Packer fans from Shiocton enjoyed the Vince Lombardi years. Russell, Carl, Tom, and Russell Obermeier went to all the Packer games played at Green Bay during the 10-year period of 1958-1968. I went to some of the games. During these years the Packers won five National Football League (NFL) championships, and they won Super Bowl I and II. Bart Starr, Paul Hornung, Jim Taylor, Henry Jordan, and Ray Nitschke were the champion players.

Pa loved Vince Lombardi and thought he was a terrific coach.

We bought our tickets on the Lambeau Field square, and they cost us $20-25 each. We actually bought tickets from other Packer fans, selling their tickets to make a profit.

Russell Obermeier usually didn't buy a ticket. He dressed up like an official and walked right through the newsroom or ticket room with no questions asked. He was a card. Sometimes he posed as a vendor selling peanuts or popcorn.

The Green Bay Packers were actually a crummy team in 1954. They played their games in an old City Stadium with wooden seats and no restrooms. The Packers were in danger of losing their franchise. The old City Stadium was an eyesore and no game was going to be played there. The players and fans longed for a game to be played in Green Bay. They needed a new stadium.

Green Bay voters decided to change this situation by approving a referendum to build a new City Stadium in 1957. Once this happened and a first game was played in Green Bay, everyone became high-spirited. Fans now were able to go to a game in Green Bay, the players had home field advantage, and the franchise was saved. When they beat the Chicago Bears, 21-17, in a stadium providing seats close to the field, plenty of parking, and restrooms, the stadium and the team became popular.

The stadium was named Lambeau Field in 1965, following the death of the coach and founder, Curly Lambeau.

Vince Lombardi became coach in 1959. To him, winning was everything. The Packers won five titles under Vince. They won three NFL Championships in 1961, 1962, and 1965. They gave their best beating to the Chicago Bears, 49-0, on September 30, 1962. They won Super Bowl I-II in 1966 and 1967.

The Packers won their first NFL title game in Green Bay in 1961. Paul Hornung scored four touchdowns to beat the Baltimore Colts, 45-7, the most points in any one Packer's game in history. Hornung came back a few weeks later to run 89 yards and score 19 points to win the NFL Championship by defeating the New York Giants, 37-0, and was named the game's outstanding player.

The most historic battle on the Frozen Tundra was the Ice Bowl occurring on December 31, 1967, when the Packers beat the Dallas Cowboys, 21-17, fighting frostbite with the weather 13 degrees below zero and a minus 46 degrees chill factor. They won with Bart Starr's historic one-yard sneak in the last 13 seconds. It was the best touchdown in Packer history. The warmest place there on this historic day was in the restrooms.

When they won the 1962 NFL Championship, the

Green Bay Packers team players claimed it was colder in New York than it had been during the Ice Bowl battle. The Packers led the whole game in New York during 13 degrees temperatures with 40 mph winds. They named Ray Nitschke their most valuable player and called him a one-man wrecking crew. They won 16-7.

In a field with four inches of fresh snow, the Pack took the 1965 NFL Championship by beating the Cleveland Browns, 23-12, at Lambeau Field. Bart Starr led the team in the third quarter with an 11-play, 90-yard drive. Paul Hornung rushed 105 yards and Jim Taylor 96 yards.

The Pack came back in 1966 and 1967 to win the NFL Championship in both years. The Packers are the only team to have won three straight championships in a row. Bart Starr shined in the 1965 game when they beat the Dallas Cowboys, 34-27, at the Cotton Bowl in Dallas. In 1967 they defeated the Dallas Cowboys again, 21-17, during the Ice Bowl.

At the end of the Ice Bowl game everyone went nuts. They mobbed the field. Coach Lombardi lost his hat to the crowd. They tore down the goal post and danced around it. All of the whiskey bottles collected amounted up to a pile five feet high and 10 feet in circumference. The bars in Green Bay were open well into the morning hours.

Green Bay was dubbed Title Town USA, and the Vince Lombardi Trophy became a reality.

Vince Lombardi said Forrest Gregg, offensive tackle, was one of the finest players he ever coached. He played 187 consecutive games, a team record.

Paul Hornung had the most points in a season with 176 in 1960. He earned a total of 760 career points, ranking third in team history.

Bart Starr was named Most Valuable Player (MVP) in Super Bowls I and II. He held the Packers career record at this time for games played, 196.

Jim Taylor led the league in 1962 with rushing and scoring 19 touchdowns.

Words cannot describe the excitement of the fans and players of the Green Bay Packers as champions in the 1960's. Bart Starr was the greatest quarterback in NFL history.

MEMORIES

I remember watching the "Noon Show."
I remember watching a soap opera so exciting we had to see every daily episode.

Sands Through the Hourglass

We turned on the TV at noon everyday to watch "The Noon Show" and turned the TV off when it was done. "The Noon Show" was fun to watch. It had a variety of offerings, including news, weather, sports, and music by some local talent. As soon as it was finished, though, off went the TV.

A big change occurred, however, in 1965. A new soap opera premiered on November 8, 1965, and we just had to watch it because it had such a good storyline. Mary even motivated Ma to watch it. It came on right after "The Noon Show." It was the first soap opera to appear in color.

The name of the show was "Days of Our Lives." The storyline centered not only on what happens in a hospital but also what happens in a family. In fact, it was a story about a family of doctors. The show concerned itself with the lives of professionals in Salem, a middle-America town, going through problems associated with love, marriage, divorce, and family life. The family underwent difficulties but wasn't consumed by them. Reverence for family and visions of a more desirable world were paramount.

The doctor family was the Horton family, led by Dr. Tom Horton and his homemaker wife Alice, with children Mickey, Bill, Addie, Marie, and Tom Jr. "Tommy." Addie and

Tommy were twins.

The show ran for 30 minute segments daily and had a cast of 11 actors. We scheduled our activities around the show. We didn't want to miss an episode.

Macdonald Carey played the role of Dr. Tom Horton, and Frances Reid played Alice. The beginning of the show each day began with Carey's words, "Like sands through the hourglass, so are the days of our lives."

Tom and Alice Horton shared a deep love, strong and solid, with a caring respect for each other, their marriage, and family. The family had trauma but not Tom and Alice. Alice is stable, condoning, cheerful, confident. Everybody liked to go over to Alice's to sample her homemade delicious donuts. Tom is fervent and just, a wise counselor, a fixer.

Out of "Day of Our Lives" comes a base of good family values. The family gives love and protection. The show gave the first showing of the devil on daytime TV, but love and decency win over evil.

Tommy died in the Korean War in 1953.

Addie married Ben Olson. His father was the richest man in Salem. Addie and Ben had two children, Steven and Julie, teenagers as the story began in 1965.

Mickey, at age 33, had become an attorney and was an eligible bachelor. He stopped over at his parents' place often for dinner and a game of chess.

Twenty-five year old Bill was finishing up his studies at Harvard Medical School.

Marie, the baby of the family, studied biochemistry at Salem University and planned to marry Tony Merritt.

As a teenager, Julie, Addie's daughter, was an attention seeker and a rebel. She got caught stealing a fur piece at a department store. Julie claimed she didn't steal it. It was just a joke. When reprimanded about it by Mickey and her dad, Julie became defiant.

Tony learned he had a fatal blood disease. It worried him, and he worried about Marie reacting to it. Tony decided to keep it a secret and broke his engagement with Marie. Marie became devastated and tried to commit suicide with an overdose of sleeping pills.

The Horton's had a tradition of hanging Christmas ornaments, actually decorated balls with family names on them, fragile and colorful, on their Christmas tree. They made a ceremony of hanging the ornaments, each family member taking a turn in hanging their ornament and saying some sentimental or cheerful words for the season.

In addition to the hanging of the ornaments, the Christmas story was read by a family member, close friend of the family, or even Santa Claus. The reader was hand picked by Alice Horton.

Marie recovered and found comfort with Craig Merritt, Tony's father, a lonely widower twice her age. Marie married Craig.

When Julie's parents moved to Europe, Julie lived with her grandparents. Julie tried Alice's and Tom's patience as no one else was able to do.

Julie got involved with David Martin, a guy somewhat older than her. They shared a common bond: neither felt they were really loved. They were going to elope, but after Tom talked to Julie about love and life, she cancelled out on it.

Susan Hunter met up with David, they made love, and she got pregnant. They didn't love each other but married for the child's sake. They intended to give the child up for adoption and then get divorced.

Julie believed David still loved her.

Tony became cured of his illness and told his dad Craig why he walked out on Marie. Marie miscarried their child and suffered postpartum depression. Craig felt to be an obstacle to the true love of the two he loved most, Tony and Marie. Craig claimed never to have loved Marie and asked for a divorce from Marie. Marie felt guilty but Craig convinced her to divorce him. She didn't accept his offer though of the house and alimony.

Alice knew Craig truly loved Marie, but Marie refused counsel. Marie moved into the Horton household.

Craig went back to his flying career to overcome his loss. He never stopped loving her. He flew his airplane far away in Asia, China, and Indonesia.

Tony began dating Marie again, trying to rebuild their love relationship.

Susan got David to put in for a transfer. The plan was to have the baby, give it up for adoption, and tell the parents it was stillborn. They hated each other and having to live together.

Bill received a job offer at Johns Hopkins Medical Center but declined in order to be able to stay in Salem. He had become interested in the psychiatry intern, Dr. Laura Spencer.

Susan Martin hemorrhaged severely, and a premature baby boy was born by Cesarean section. The crisis brought Susan's parents to her side and drew Susan and David closer together. Susan bonded with her baby boy. She named him Richard "Dickie" and told David they needed to stay married for the sake of the boy. Both Susan and David told their parents the truth, and they were encouraged to be responsible parents.

Julie, still loving David and having hopes of marrying him, became belligerent to Susan. Tom wanted to send Julie to Paris to live with her parents, but she moved to an apartment.

The Horton household went into conflict as well. Mickey and Bill became rivals, and Tom was unable to settle their differences. Alice had told Tony how his actions to Marie were never to be forgotten. Tony left Salem, and Marie started working at University Hospital. Bill developed tuberculosis of the hand and wasn't able to do surgery anymore. Bill left town to work in another medical facility.

David grew attached to his son and resisted Julie. David felt Susan was overprotective of Dickie and started spending more time with him at the park without Susan.

One day at the park Dickie fell out of a swing and struck his head. He died a week later. Soon afterwards Susan shot and killed David. Through the efforts of Mickey and Laura Spencer, Susan was judged not guilty of murder on the basis of temporary insanity. David's mother soon after shot Susan and left her to be a semi-invalid with a serious heart problem. David's father forgave Susan and helped her recover.

Bill came back to Salem, but Laura no longer wanted to marry him. She became engaged to Bill's brother Mickey instead, and they wed.

Bill had surgery again on his hand in order to regain total control of his hand. He conquered his fears and once again became a surgeon, his chosen career.

The story ends here for now, only to be continued…

And so, "like sands in the hourglass, so are the days of our lives…"

MEMORIES

I remember the family growing by leaps and bounds.
I remember going to dances.
I remember meeting a charming young lady at a Halloween dance.
I remember parking under the cherry tree at Ervida's parents homestead in DePere.

An Enchanting Halloween

I didn't have a girlfriend yet. I had a few dates but nothing developed into anything serious. I had taken Margo Bergstresser to the 1956 Junior Prom, "Blue Hawaii" at Shiocton High School. I had dated a couple girls at OSC. I had dated my friend Beaver Lemere's cousin Darlene for a couple years and even gave her my class ring, but it wasn't a lasting relationship.

Five of my brothers were married and building their families. Donnie and Marvella had six children, Ricky, Sharon, Darla, Karla, Greg, and Cynthia. Cynthia died at an early age. Roger and Gerry had four boys, Stevie, Brucie, Kevin, and Dean. Gerald and Arlene had six children, Randy, Diane, Doug, Helen, Wayne, and Jenny. Helen died at an early age. Carl and Barbara had nine children, David, Darrell, Duane, Debbie, Dennis, Dawn, Dale, Donna, and Dusty. Russell and Gerri had Jeff, Laurie, Stephanie, and Andy.

Russell came most weekends with Jeff to visit at Grandma's.

Roger's lived on the farm next door and Carl's in a trailer on the lawn south of our house. I, therefore, saw Stevie, Brucie, David, Darrell, Duane, and other nephews and nieces in the back yard. Pa had purchased the play equipment from the school system and set it up in our back yard.

Many of my classmates had married and were building their families, too. Judy Johnson married Jack Tackman, and they had four children, Tom, Jolene, Theresa, and Jeannie. Cousin Maxine Miller married Joe Buss, and they had seven children, Bruce, Bill, Brad, Bridget, Becky, Boyd, and Bonnie. Cousin Tom Van Straten married my classmate Janice Conradt and they had five children, Larry, Bobby, Pam, Nicky, and Rodney. Cousin Bobbe Mae Van Straten married David Robinson and they had two children, Jeff and Jill. Cousin Norita Van Straten married Gary Barrington and they had seven children, Debbie, Brad, Bart, Bryan, Dawn, Denise, and Benjamin. That's just a few. Many more, and growing.

I longed for love and for a commitment.

Dances and dancing was one of our favorite types of entertainment. We had at least one dance to go to each weekend-- Saturday night dances, community dances, barroom dances, wedding dances, teen dances, plus Christmas dances, and Halloween dances. Even after television became the norm, dances continued to be popular.

The Shiocton Community Club sponsored a Halloween dance on October 30, 1965, and I decided to go to it. I made a Halloween costume to wear. I wore a mask made up from one of Ma's old nylon stockings. It is amazing how stretching a nylon stocking over one's head completely distorts your facial features. No one was going to recognize me. The rest of the costume consisted of an old, wrinkled, olive-green hat, a purple turtleneck shirt, rags tied around my pants, and an old, gray coat.

The Halloween party was held at the American Legion Clubhouse.

I went directly into the barroom and stood in front of my cousin Carol Sommers. Jack Andrews stood nearby. I didn't speak a word. I didn't utter a sound. To do so was only to end up identifying myself. I wanted to remain unknown as long as possible. It wasn't long though before they discovered the mystery guy in the costume.

The next thing I knew everyone was going out to the dance floor. I followed suit. When couples began parading around the dance floor to compete for best costumes, a lady in costume grabbed my arm and motioned for us to masquerade around the floor, too. We won a prize.

After the masquerade ended, dancing began. We danced, and she taught me to do the two step. We danced the rest of the night until the music stopped.

This young lady wore large overalls, big oversized shoes, fake glasses with a big nose, and a straw hat. As everyone knows, beauty is only skin deep, but nonetheless I was able to see there was a beautiful young woman behind the costume.

I asked her about taking her home. She checked me out first with her friends, and they said I was an ok guy. So we took off. I took a little detour before taking her home. We stopped at a bar on the south end of town. When I finally had pulled up by her residence, I neglected to take her to the door.

She lived in an upstairs apartment at Mrs. Rueden's across from Dr. La Croix's.

I found out her name was Ervida Carpenter. She taught third grade at the Shiocton school system. Her parents, Donald and Phyllis Carpenter, and brother Larry lived in DePere, WI, on Lawrence Drive south of State Hwy. 41.

I had fun with Ervida the night of the Halloween dance, and I think she fun, too. I was attracted to her and fascinated with her. I wanted to see her again. Did she like me? Did I have a chance with her? Was she the one for me and was I the one for her?

I just thought about her and dreamed of her, being the bashful kind of guy I was during this time of my life. I did see Ervida a few times though as she and her teacher roommate Marilyn Mrotek walked by Gug's filling station as I worked.

Marilyn Mrotek

One day Mrs. Kroner decided to play cupid. When she stopped at Gug's filling station for gas on a day I was working, she told me Ervida was a wonderful young lady and invited me to come over to the bowling alley in Black Creek on a night the teachers bowled.

I did go over to the bowling alley on teachers' night. I remember the night. It was November 18, 1965. Ervida was part of the Shiocton teachers' league bowling on this night. It had been two weeks since Ervida and I met. She rode home to Shiocton with me afterwards, and we stopped at a restaurant for a bite to eat before going to her apartment. This time I was a gentleman, opening the car doors for her and taking her to the door leading up to her apartment. We set a time for another date. After this encounter, we went on one date after another.

I now had a girlfriend, and Ervida had a boyfriend.

We went to the bars in Shiocton because this was where everyone got together to have fun. We danced at the bars. We attended school events. We went to the movies at the Seymour theater, the New London theaters, and the Appleton theaters. We went bowling in Black Creek and New London. We went to weddings because someone was always getting married.

The bars and bowling alleys reeked with smoke. We found a different place to go to in order to avoid the smoky atmosphere. We began going to the dances at the Cinderella Ballroom in Appleton on Saturday nights. We danced the circle step, the bunny hop, and the Flying Dutchman.

After you have been dating for a period of time, you get to meet the parents and other members of the family.

My parents met Ervida at one of the weddings we attended or at a school event, like a basketball game. She met some of the other members of my family as well at one of these events or at the bars.

I met Ervida's parents, Don and Peggy Carpenter, at their home in DePere. We walked in the front door. Her mother was sitting at the table in the kitchen. You were able to see her through the peep-hole, a hole cut into the wall between the kitchen and the living room. Her brother Larry had an embarrassing moment when I first met him. He said, "Hi Dan, I'm Ervida's sister." Ervida took me out to the barn to meet her dad.

When we came to the Carpenter homestead, morning, daytime, or night, we parked by the barn milkhouse under the cherry tree. We always parked under the cherry tree at night and talked. On some occasions, Larry came home and walked down by the cherry tree for a chat with us.

Peggy and Don Carpenter

Larry Carpenter
Photo courtesy of Chuck Leininger

Carpenter family (1965)

Ervida (1962)
Photo courtesy of Chuck Leininger

The Carpenter Homestead

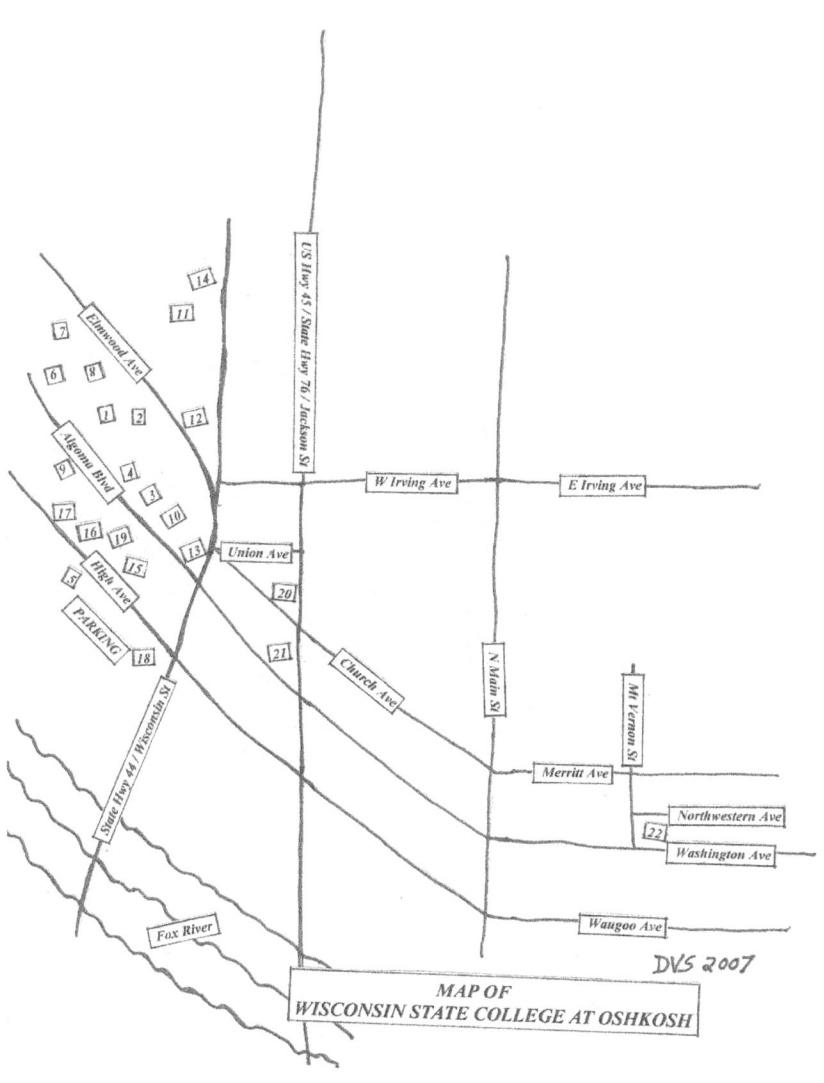

WSC CAMPUS (AND VICINITY) MAP KEY

1. Dempsey Hall (1917)
2. Old Gym (1908) / Forrest R. Polk Library (1962)
3. Reeve Memorial Union (1959)
4. Albee Hall (1954)
5. Kolf Sports Center (1971)
6. Rose C. Swart Training School (1929) / Swart Hall
7. Halsey Science Center (1963/1967)
8. Harrington Hall (1913)
9. Radford Hall (1951)
10. Clemans Hall (1960)
11. Evans Hall (1965)
12. Fletcher Hall (1964)
13. Nelson Hall (1965)
14. Stewart Hall (1965)
15. Taylor Hall (1963)
16. Webster Hall (1958)
17. Donner Hall (1964)
18. Gruenhagen Hall (1966)
19. Pollock House (1943)
20. Mary Brahe House (515 Jackson Street)
21. Winnebago County Court House (415 Jackson Street)
22. Oshkosh Public Library (106 Washington Avenue)

MEMORIES

I remember commuting to OSC during my senior year.
I remember using the GI Bill.
I remember getting on the Dean's List and honor roll.
I remember graduating from OSC.

A Whiz of a Senior

I last attended OSC in January, 1961, when I withdrew from all my second semester courses. Many changes had occurred at the college during the past five years.

The college name changed again. It was Wisconsin State College at Oshkosh in 1966 and changed to Wisconsin State University at Oshkosh in 1967, with the WSC-O logo in 1966 and the WSU-O logo in 1967. The old name continued to be used though-- Oshkosh State or OSC.

The campus had grown. The library was no longer located on the second floor of Dempsey Hall but contained in a building all its own called the Forrest R. Polk Library. The Halsey Science Center was new, construction started in 1963. More residence halls had been added, including Evans Hall, Fletcher Hall, Nelson Hall, Stewart Hall, Taylor Hall, Donner Hall, and Gruenhagen Hall. A large, open parking lot had been added off of High Avenue. I used this new parking lot often during my senior year at OSC.

I commuted to Oshkosh during my last year of

undergraduate studies at Oshkosh State. I lived at home in Shiocton. I stopped over at Mrs. Brahe's occasionally to visit. I told her I was attending college again at OSC, studying to be a librarian, and commuting from Shiocton. She said I was welcome to stay over anytime it became necessary.

My chances for success in my studies this year were most promising. I had a goal ever before me of becoming a librarian, and I had a steady girlfriend.

I whizzed through all my courses and requirements for college graduation. I attended school the entire year of 1966, winter, summer, fall.

Although I had earned and saved money for this year of college, I did some work at Gug's filling station and Uncle Mike Miller's grocery store. I helped out on the farm, too.

I received assistance from Uncle Sam, too. I applied for educational assistance under the GI Bill and was awarded 31 months of educational entitlement. I used the GI Bill for seven months-- two months in the summer of 1966 at $75 per month and five months in the fall semester at $100 per month.

I stopped at the Shiocton Post Office often during the time I attended college in 1966. Aunt Erna and Aunt Grace waited on me and sometimes Percy Braatz. My aunts gave me lots of sage advice during my post office visits.

Achieving B grades in two off-campus summer school courses during the summer of 1965 had guaranteed my re-admittance to Oshkosh State. I had completed all the paper work with my adviser to resume my studies at Oshkosh State in January, 1966.

Janet Schwenn

Sally Teresinski

Helen Wahoski

Dorothy Martin

    I registered to take six courses, three credits each, 18 credits total. The courses were: Library Science 211 (Book Selection) taught by Janet Schwenn; Library Science 209 (Teaching of Books and Librarianship) taught by Sally Teresinski; Library Science 214 (Reading Interests of Adults) taught by Helen Wahoski; English 112 (Literature for Children) taught by Ray Schroeder; English 245 (Elizabethan Jacobean Literature) taught by Dorothy Martin; and, English 251 (American Novel) teacher unrecalled.

    In the Book Selection course, I, the library student,

learned Carter and Bonk's *Building Library Collections* top, bottom, and sideways, as well as Shores' *Basic Reference Sources* and Winchell's *Guide to Reference Sources*. The principles, standards, and factors of book selection, statements of library purposes, censorship ("The Library Bill of Rights"), policy statements, the profile of a book selector, annotations, and book reviews and evaluations became a part of my fiber. I learned how to select books by subject and by type of material. The physical aspects (format, textual material, et cetera) of books, special selection problems (relating to editions, translations, series, and gifts), surveying and weeding collections, and surveying the community were all covered, as well as the publishing trade, order work, the trade bibliography (*CBI, PTLA, Publishers Weekly, and BIP*), book selection aids (*Book Review Digest, Fiction Catalog*, and *Standard Catalog*), and reviewing sources.

The Reading Interests of Adults course acquainted me with the aims of the public library and principles to follow when talking about books. I was exposed to several reading lists of books, including the "Notable Books of ..." lists. We reviewed books by format (fiction, non-fiction) and by type within each format. Progress exams in this course consisted mostly of matching authors to their books and some essay questions.

In the children's literature course we studied May Hill Arbuthnot's *Children and Books* cover to cover, and complemented it with the thorough usage of the *Children's Catalog*, Kunitz' *Junior Book of Authors*, Brewton's *Index to Children's Poetry*, *Book Review Digest*, and the *Horn Book*. We studied the history of children's books. We learned how to evaluate and select children's books. We covered the children's books categories of Mother Goose, folk tales, fables, myths, epics, fairy tales, the U.S. and other lands and peoples, animal stories, biography, poetry, and historical fiction. We learned about introducing books to children and what books children need to read. We reviewed books and authors winners of Newbery and Caldecott medals. We had to read at least one Caldecott and one Newbery book. I read numerous children's books in this course, many I never read as a child. Many of these were a fast read. It was a great adventure. We were required to make up note cards on books read. During some class hours we moved our chairs in a round to discuss books read.

This turned out to be my best semester for overall achievement. I earned four A's and two B's, achieving a grade point average of 3.33, my highest ever. I achieved a B+ average and was placed on the Dean's list and the spring honor roll. Can you imagine? Four A's!

I registered to take three courses during the summer school session of 1966. The courses were: Health Education 6 (First Aid), one credit; Library Science 82 (Library Materials), two credits; and, Sociology 101 (Principles of Sociology), three credits. I did well in summer school, too, earning an A in the first aid course and B's in the other two courses. I had failed the first aid course in 1960.

In the library materials course we learned about the history of books and printing, type style and design, types of printing presses, types of printing, book binding, and conserving library materials. We studied buying lists and catalogs for building a basic book collection.

I registered for a full course load again of 18 credits during the fall semester of 1966, my final semester. This time I was taking seven courses. Four of them were three-credit courses and three were two-credit courses. The courses included: Literature for Adolescents (65307) taught by Ray Schroeder; Library Operations and Management (65101); Library in the Community (65509) taught by Jerry Shea; Library Practice (65707); Cataloging and Classification (65311) taught by Marion Archer; School Library Administration (65701) taught by Helen Wahoski; and, Multi-Sensory Aids (85501) taught by Frederick Mundt.

Frederick Mundt **Marion Archer**

In the literature course for adolescents we studied the reading interests of adolescents and how to select books to satisfy their reading interests. We studied authors and their contributions to literature in the categories of school and sports, hobbies, careers, romance, home and family life, other lands and peoples, historical fiction, humor, poetry, essays, science fiction, controversial fiction, and animal stories. Our class assignments consisted of preparing for and giving 10-minute book talks in each of those categories. We had several reading lists to choose from. We sat with our chairs arranged in a circle during the book talk sessions.

I read and gave book talks in class on Henry Miller's *Tropic of Cancer*, Annis Duff's *Longer Flight*, Rosamond DuJardin's *Senior Prom*, Maureen Daly's *Seventeenth Summer*, George Orwell's *Animal Farm* and *Nineteen Eighty-Four*, John Steinbeck's *Of Mice and Men*, Jerome Salinger's *The Catcher in the Rye*, William Golding's *Lord of the Flies*, Mary O'Hara's *Green Grass of Wyoming* and *My Friend Flicka*, Aldous Huxley's *Brave New World*, Henry David Thoreau's *Walden*, Frank B. Gilbreth Jr.'s *Cheaper by the Dozen*, and Nelle Harper Lee's *To Kill a Mockingbird*.

Ray Schroeder's class on adolescent literature was exciting, and I enjoyed the exposure to some terrific literature not only through the books I read but also the books the other classmates read and talked about. We read or talked about or had reading lists for every children's book ever written in Ray Schroeder's class, including the Newbery and Caldecott Medal winners and many more.

What happened to the *Tropics*? One day I looked for my *Tropics* books I had checked out from the university's library. Henry Miller's *Tropic of Cancer* and *Tropic of Capricorn*. I needed to give a book talk on one of them in Ray Schroeder's lit class in a couple days. I asked Ma if she had moved them. Oh, boy, I was in for it. Ma told me she had taken them and hid them. She didn't want those dirty, filthy books sitting around the house and reading them was bound to thwart a young man's mind and cause him to have an unsavory attitude to sex and marriage. I told her I planned to take them back the next day and had plans to use another book for my report. Actually, I had to report on one of them, unknown to Ma. I drove up on County Trk M and read *The Tropic of Cancer*, sitting in my car reading and taking notes. I talked to Mr. Schroeder about it the next day. He understood Ma's viewpoint on the issue but also stressed that a librarian needs to adhere to the Library Bill of Rights and not censor any book from the reading public. I understood Ma's viewpoint, too, as well as my responsibility to make any book available to the library user regardless of content. Parents, not the library, need to pay attention to and put limits on what young people read.

In the School Library Administration course we studied the role of the school library, the aims of the school library, and the selection of books for it. We were exposed to the School Library Bill of Rights. We learned about school library objectives, the duties of student assistants, ordering procedures, and school library floor plans (building plans).

I didn't make the Dean's List this last semester because I only received a passing grade in the multi-sensory aids course. I earned two A's and four B's in the other courses.

Even though I only passed the multi-sensory aids course, I learned how to operate tape recorders (using reels) and movie projectors. I was prepared to operate these multi-sensory machines on the job, if necessary.

My library science and English classes put the polishing touch on my education by schooling me in the reading interests of library users, the ready reference tools to use in a library, and the techniques of cataloging library materials.

Marion Fuller Archer fully motivated me to complete my studies in library science and to become a library cataloger. Her cataloging class was awesome for me. Mrs. Archer was an excellent teacher, cataloger, and author of children's books. During this semester and beyond she was working heavily on changing the university library's classification system from Dewey Decimal to Library of Congress.

I had an opportunity to put my education to practical use with the library practice course. I was exposed to public library work at the public service desk and in the catalog room. I was given an opportunity to actually do some original cataloging on a couple items in the catalog room. You can only imagine what a thrill this was for me. This library practice was a great experience for me and confirmed my desire to work in a public library.

An Off-Campus Event, Spring, 1966

The Shiocton High School prom, held in April, 1966, as always was an exciting event in the lives of the high school students. Among Mary's innermost circle of friends were three guys, Michael Ratsch, Jerry Pluger, and Tom Kennedy. Mary had a prom date with Tom. Ervida and I were at the farm house the night of the prom when Tom picked Mary up and gave her a corsage. They had a good time

at the farm house before even going to the prom itself. We went down to the prom, too, as spectators, and took Joyce, Alice, and Karen along. It was a thrilling evening.

Campus Spotlight, 1966-1967

I didn't have any time or opportunity to take part in or keep up with campus life events.

This was the first year in Oshkosh State's sports history for the college to have an intercollegiate gymnastics team.

The Titans had one of their best basketball seasons ever, sweeping to a conference championship with a 14-2 record and into the Wisconsin State play-off game with Lakeland College of Sheboygan.

Oshkosh State added male cheerleaders for the first time, adding new cheers and talents, color and attraction.

The Titans football team didn't do well this year. Twenty-five lettermen returned in the beginning of the season but it dwindled down to 12 by the end of season due to injuries and illness.

    My adviser informed me I had met all the requirements for graduation. Graduation was set for January 20, 1967. I rented a cap and gown from the union store for the graduation ceremonies. I stopped over to tell Mrs. Brahe of my achievements at OSC during my senior year, earning my college degree.

    Ervida and my parents came to the graduation ceremonies held inside Albee Hall. We stopped for a snack afterwards.

Boone, a 1967 OSC Graduate

A Library Interview

On January 20, 1967 I graduated from Wisconsin State University at Oshkosh, aka WSU-O, aka OSC, earning a B.S. Degree in the College of Letters and Science with a Library Science major and an English minor.

I lived at home in Shiocton until I landed a job. I didn't get a job right away.

I sent applications to 30 major libraries in the State of Wisconsin. I received no responses.

I continued working for Gug at the filling station.

Ervida and I went on dates once a week throughout the year of 1966, mostly on Saturday nights. Getting together once a week was all we were able to manage then. I had been a full-time student and Ervida a full-time teacher. Once I graduated from WSU-O though we managed to date twice a week. On Saturday nights we went dancing. During the middle of week we spent time in Ervida's apartment, went for a cruise in Shiocton environs, went to a movie, or drove over to her parents' place in DePere.

Ervida and I had developed strong feelings for each other. We had fallen in love with each other.

I wanted to propose marriage to Ervida, but I held off doing it because I needed the security of steady job. I needed job security.

Mary was looking forward to high school graduation and attending college. She liked home economics with a passion and was encouraged by her home economics teacher,

Mary, a Shiocton High School graduate, 1967
Picture Courtesy of F.J. Pechman

Mrs. Powers, to study home economics at the Stevens Point university.

Mary was the DAR Good Citizen representative during her senior year of high school, based on attributes of leadership, character, patriotism, and dependability. Mary had been active in Library Club work, FHA, and Drama Club. She held four class offices.

When I sent follow-up letters to the 30 Wisconsin libraries, I received a call from Mr. E.R. Kunert, Director of the Mead Public Library, Sheboygan, WI. He set an interview with me for Friday, May 26, 1967.

Mead Public Library had a great reputation as one of the best libraries in the State of Wisconsin. I felt honored to be considered for a job at this library.

I told my parents and Ervida how excited I was about this job opportunity. They were comfortable with my intentions of taking this job.

The interview went great, and I got the job. Mr. Kunert had now become my boss, setting my starting work day the following Monday, May 29, 1967. He offered to give me any assistance needed in locating a place of residence. I found an apartment to rent within an hour after the interview ended and headed home to Shiocton afterwards.

I packed on Saturday and left for Sheboygan Sunday afternoon, after spending time with family and Ervida.

I enjoyed working at the library. I worked Monday nights at the reference desk and the rest of the time in the catalog room.

I went home every weekend I had Saturday off.

I proposed marriage to Ervida on September 16, 1967. I was eager but Ervida wasn't. The timing was just off. She said she loved me but didn't want to be engaged just yet. She had things she wanted to be secure in, too. For one thing, she was finishing up on her studies for her college degree at OSC. We kept dating but an engagement was out of the question for now.

My Favorites

At the ripe age of 28 years, I had a few favorite things in my life destined to be tops for the rest of my life.

I loved to read. Novels with lots of action were especially appealing to me. I had a passion for science fiction novels.

My favorite actress was Carolyn Jones. Other actresses were bound to win my heart, but Carolyn Jones always remained tops with me. Her first husband was television producer Aaron Spelling. She always played bit parts or supporting roles, but I was attracted to her because of her big eyes, cute smile, and her funny witticisms. She was cast in *The Big Heat* and *House of Wax*. She appeared in *The Bachelor Party, Last Train From Gun Hill*, Elvis Presley's *King Creole*, and the television series "The Addams Family."

My favorite book was actually a tie between two books. I had read many great books, but my favorites for all time were both classics and both were made into motion pictures, William Henry Hudson's *Green Mansions: a Romance of the Tropical Forest* (1904) and Theodore Dreiser's *An American Tragedy* (1925).

I first came upon *Green Mansions* in the sixth grade. I bought the Classics Illustrated Comic Book of the book and was so thrilled with it. I drew a picture of the bird girl Rima, and my teacher, Mrs. Kroner, posted it up on the board. Mrs. Kroner posted all the good art work by her students on the board. Later I read the book and then I saw the movie in 1959, adapted from the book.

    The romance story of *Green Mansions* was about a young traveler named Abel discovering an enchanted forest in the Guyana jungle of southeastern Venezuela and encountering there the girl named Rima. He hears strange bird-like singing in the forest and finds out the sounds are made by Rima. The local native Indians avoid the forest because they think Rima is an evil spirit. They call her "the daughter of the Didi." They had chased her up a giant tree and fired a dart at her, but she caught it and threw it back down, killing one of them. They didn't go into the forest after this occurrence. After Abel is bitten by a coral snake, he is taken to a hut and healed. Rima lives in the hut with her protector, a man named Nuflo. After he recovers, Abel spends time in the forest with Rima. She flits to and fro and conceals herself well within the trees of the forest. Abel is often unable to find her. Abel falls in love with Rima, but she is a stranger to white men and he cannot speak her unknown language. Rima is a vegetarian and won't tolerate the killing of animals for food. Nuflo had gone off one day and killed one of his dogs for food. He needed meat so bad. Riolama is actually Rima's real name. She came from a place called Riolama. Abel and Rima talk Nuflo into taking them to Riolama. Rima learns about her people and then hurries back to the forest ahead of Abel and Nuflo. The Indians, upon discovering Rima's absence, had ventured back into the enchanted forest. When they saw Rima return, they chased her back up the giant tree, but this time, instead of shooting a dart at her, they burned up the giant tree and Rima with it as well and burned the hut, too. Abel retaliates by killing the enemy tribe. Abel collects Rima's ashes with him as he departs from the enchanted forest. The motion picture starred Audrey Hepburn as Rima, Anthony Perkins as Abel, and Lee J. Cobb as Nuflo. Mel Ferrer, Audrey Hepburn's husband, directed the film.

The story of *An American Tragedy* is one of a young man named Clyde Griffiths having troublesome relationships with women. As he grew up in Kansas City, his poor, religious parents forced him to participate in their street missionary work. He gets a job as a bellboy at a local hotel, but when he kills a young child with a stolen car, he flees first to Chicago and then to the fictional town of Lycurgus, New York. He becomes a foreman at a wealthy uncle's collar factory and is attracted to a poor, innocent farm girl named Roberta Alden working under him. He has sex with her but realizes he won't ever be able to marry her. He also develops a relationship with the wealthy Sondra Finchley, and Roberta discovers she is pregnant. Roberta threatens to expose him if Clyde doesn't marry her, and Clyde plans to do Roberta in and make it look accidental. Clyde takes her on a canoe ride, capsizes the canoe, and lets her drown. Following a sensational trial, Clyde is convicted of murder and executed.

The film *A Place in the Sun* (1951) is based on the last part of the novel by Dreiser but the names are different. Montgomery Clift plays George Eastman, Shelley Winters plays Alice Tripp, the homely girl, and Elizabeth Taylor plays the elegant Angela Vickers. George has a scandalous relationship with Alice Tripp and falls in love with the beautiful Angela Vickers. George has the idea of dropping a lesser life with Alice for a better life with Angela, but Alice is not going to let him get away with it, being pregnant with his baby. The movie ends the same, with George drowning Alice, a sensational court trial, conviction, and execution.

Both books and movies were a thrill to me. These were such terrific writers. The movie reviews were poor, but still I thoroughly enjoyed watching them.

Our Home

The barn, silo, shed, and house hidden by the tree in the picture's background were Ed and Minnie Johnson's home buildings.

The Farm House (front side)

The Farm House (back side)

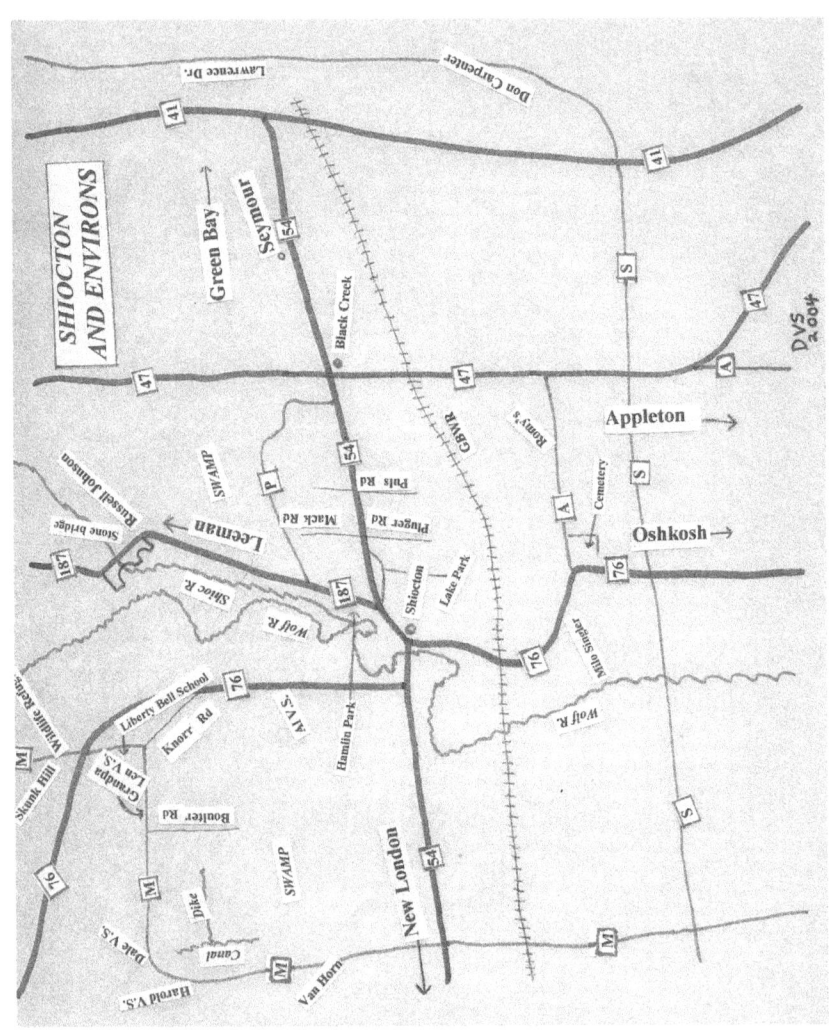

A map of Shiocton and environs

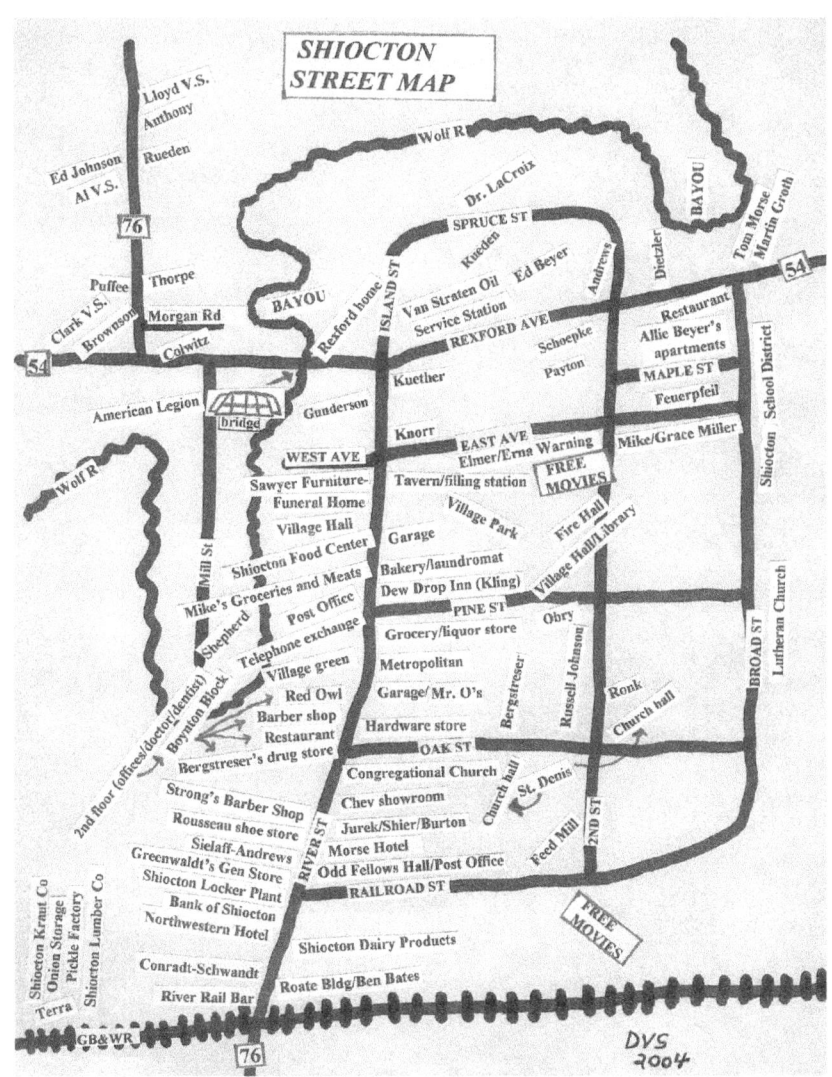

A Shiocton streets map

Errata : Corrections on the *Schemer* Facts

The author became aware of errors in some written facts in *Schemer* after it went to press.

The barn, silo, shed, and house hidden by the tree in the picture's background on page 8 were Ed and Minnie Johnson's home buildings.

The first line of the third paragraph on page 35 should read: "Grandpa's parents Martin and Gertrude (Vanderwise)"

The third word of the third line on page 45 should read: Marlon.

Facts about the last paragraph on page 92: Carl quit high school during Christmas break in his senior year, his twelfth year of school.

Facts about the last paragraph on page 94: Dale and Phyllis actually were not my uncle and aunt. Dale was my second cousin, but I always thought of them as my uncle and aunt. Carl's godparents were Uncle Clark and Aunt Erna, not Uncle Henry and Aunt Agnes.

The last sentence in the fifth paragraph on page 99 should read: "Some steamboats sank in an area known as Steamboat Bayou, located southwest of Hamlin Park."

Facts about the fifth paragraph on page 108: The Ed Rueden family included more than three children, more than Roger, Betty, and Joann. There were also Cecilia, Ervin, Millie, Marion, and Agnes.

Facts about the second paragraph on page 160: Aunt Marian wasn't my aunt. Her husband Lloyd was my second cousin. All of Uncle Hank's children, Harold, Dale, Raymond, Roy, Catherine, Irene, Frances, Helen, Lloyd, and Margaret, were my second cousins.

The first sentence of the third paragraph on page 188 should read: "Gordie Collar tried it on the Fourth of July."

The first sentence of the fourth paragraph on page 193 should read: "Our sleds had steel runners."

The last sentence on page 210 should read: "I remember picking beans in long, slender bags at Lloyd's."

The sentence on line five of the second paragraph on page 212 should read: "We picked beans at Lloyd's."

Facts about the fourth paragraph on page 227: Carl is a whiz at this and got the correct facts to me on this one. All of our Massey-Harris tractors had electric starters, not hand cranks. The tractor we hand-cranked was the Allis-Chalmers.

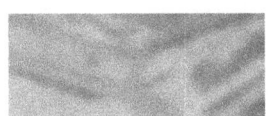

Glen Outlook Publishing, Daniel Glen Van Straten
3633 S 17th PL, Sheboygan, WI 53081
dgjvanstraten@aol.com

Praise for *Schemer*

What fun reading your story! I enjoyed every minute of your telling and could often relate and even remember. I like your uncomplicated and gentle way of explaining how things were; mixed with your humor and your gentle nature, it was enchanting. And then the illustrations - they are phenomenal, so whimsical and cheerful. I could see libraries and other public places wanting to display them. So many of us Van Stratens love to use the written word to communicate - that runs in the family. I don't often bump into a relative who is an artist. The drawings are charming. And the family photos - such memories! Bravo all around. A wonderful gift to others, and an even more special gift to yourself, I know from experience!

    -Donna Van Straten Remmert, a first cousin, author of *The Littlest Big Kid* and *The Jitterbug Girl*

I just wanted to share a couple of "zingers." I like your I Remember format a lot. I didn't know "Silver Thread Among the Gold" originated in Shiocton. Love the song. Joe McCarthy was a friend of Bill Lucht and we have poker chips his hands have touched. He graduated from Larry and my high school in 2 1/2 years while working at the local drug store. What a great brain. What a sad life. I enjoyed your "walking" the streets of Shiocton. Did you know there is no longer a grocery store there? Residents have to go to New London. My hometown of Manawa is similar. So many changing "faces" on Main Street. All you said about the Fabulous Fifties was so special. By the way, we have a 16-party line! When my dad wanted to call the vet or the breeder, he shouted a few ---- words and our neighbor and his sister cleared the line instantly! Our daughter was a meteorologist for WBAY for

12-15 years. I'm reading and enjoying---and relating.
    -Sandi Lucht, wife of first cousin Larry Lucht

... your book ... the entire thing is fun to read. I like the illustrations very much....they add a lot to the story. And of course the pictures are all wonderful, too. I can tell you put a great deal of effort into your book, and it's delightful!
    -Joan Laffey Roloff, first cousin, author of *Saving Grace*

 I just finished reading your book, and I want to tell you how much I enjoyed it. The book brought back so many wonderful memories to me. I am close to the same age as you and grew up on a dairy farm near Five Corners in the town of Lima, Sheboygan County. My family was also of Dutch background and lived very much the same way as yours did. Your pictures of the old school looked much like the Oostburg High School in the '50's. Your description of the food and canning reminded me of my mother's canning stuff and recipes of canned tomatoes, peaches, beets, peach jam, and so forth. Those were "the good old days" and we certainly had to work hard picking and weeding all those vegetables. Keep on writing.
    -Mary L. DuMez, retired Oostburg librarian

Thank you for the wonderful book you wrote. When I heard about it, I knew I had to read it. Knowing your Dutch farm background, I knew I would truly be able to relate to it. I grew up on the DePagter farm passed on by my grandpa in 1868. The outdoor outhouses, no electricity, no telephone, getting up during storms, hazardous filling of silos, tipping outhouses on Halloween, shoe stringing potatoes (we called it ricing potatoes), the 40 acre farm (ours was too), selling Vaseline (I sold seeds), big gardens, the songs and movies you mentioned were the same I knew, sugar beets, and Mexicans-- reading of all these things brought back such wonderful memories. I could relate to so much. You have a great style of writing,

preserving the history, feelings, and culture of days gone by. I am looking forward to your next book.
    -June Ver Velde, retired Mead (Sheboygan) librarian

```
I've just finished reading your book, and
I'm writing to thank you for taking the
time to write it. (I came across it a few
days ago on the New Books shelf at the
Appleton Public Library.) Your enthusiasm
for life and your love for your parents
and family are evident on every page. The
occasional moments of drama such as Roger
saving Mary and you getting your lips
stuck on the Quaker State sign, and the
occasional bits of humor such as Bobbie
Mae's skirt getting torn, helped sustain
my interest and reminded me that this was
a real life, not just a story. The book
contains a wealth of information about
farm life and small town life in Wisconsin
in the 40s and 50s. As the years go by, it
will become more and more valuable as a
record of what it was like to grow up at
that time. Congratulations on a great
achievement, and thanks again for taking
the time to write the book. I enjoyed
reading it.
          -Bill Coan
```

Have read your book and enjoyed it. I know we have met since I once worked for Gerald at the station about 1969. Nice to read about my home town and so many people that I knew of which many were friends. My mother also worked with your dad at the post office and always thought very highly of him. Congrats on not only writing an enjoyable book but also being part of a very respected family in the community.
    -David Halle

Address inquiries,
with a self-addressed, stamped envelope, to:

Daniel Glen Van Straten
Glen Outlook Publishing
3633 S 17th PL
Sheboygan, WI 53081

email: dgjvanstraten@aol.com

www.ingramcontent.com/pod-product-compliance
Lightning Source LLC
Chambersburg PA
CBHW020737160426
43192CB00006B/218